Creative Learning in the Primary School

Bob Jeffrey and Peter Woods

 Routledge
Taylor & Francis Group

LONDON AND NEW YORK

First published 2009
by Routledge
2 Park Square, Milton Park, Abingdon, Oxon OX14 4RN

Simultaneously published in the USA and Canada
by Routledge
270 Madison Ave, New York, NY 10016

Routledge is an imprint of the Taylor & Francis Group, an informa business

© 2009 Bob Jeffrey and Peter Woods

Typeset in Sabon by
GreenGate Publishing Services, Tonbridge, Kent
Printed and bound in Great Britain by
CPI Antony Rowe, Chippenham, Wiltshire

British Library Cataloguing in Publication Data
A catalogue record for this book is available from the British Library

Library of Congress Cataloging in Publication Data
Jeffrey, Bob, 1946–
Creative learning in the primary school / Bob Jeffrey and Peter Woods.
p. cm.
Includes bibliographical references and index.
1. Active learning—Great Britain. 2. Creative teaching—Great Britain. 3. Teacher–student relationships—Great Britain. 4. Education, Elementary—Great Britain—Curricula. I. Woods, Peter, 1934– II. Title.
LB1027.23.J44 2009
372.1102—dc22
2008026693

ISBN10: 0-415-46471-4 (hbk)
ISBN10: 0-415-46472-2 (pbk)
ISBN10: 0-203-88473-6 (ebk)

ISBN13: 978-0-415-46471-0 (hbk)
ISBN13: 978-0-415-46472-7 (pbk)
ISBN13: 978-0-203-88473-7 (ebk)

Creative Learning in the Primary School

Creative Learning in the Primary School uses ethnographic research to consider the main features of creative teaching and learning within the context of contemporary policy reforms. In particular, the authors are interested in the clash between two oppositional discourses – creativity and performativity – and how they are resolved in creative teacher practice.

The first section of the book explores the nature of creative teaching and learning by examining four key features: relevance, control, ownership and innovation. The authors devote a chapter to each of these aspects, outlining their properties and illustrating them with a wide range of examples, mainly from recent practice in primary schools.

The second section presents some instructive examples of schools promoting creative learning, and how creative primary schools have responded to the policy reforms of recent years. The chapters focus specifically on:

- how pupils act as a powerful resource for creative learning for each other and for their teachers;
- how teachers have appropriated the reforms to enhance their creativity;
- how one school has moved over a period of ten years from heavy constraint to high creativity.

The blend of analysis, case-study material and implications for practice will make this book attractive to primary teachers, school managers, policy makers, teacher educators and researchers.

Bob Jeffrey is Research Fellow at the Department of Education, The Open University, UK.

Peter Woods is Emeritus Professor at the Department of Education, The Open University, UK.

Contents

Acknowledgements

We are grateful to Taylor & Francis Journals for their permission to include updated versions of the following articles:

> Woods, P. (1994) 'Critical students: Breakthroughs in learning.' *International Studies in the Sociology of Education*, Vol. 4(2), pp. 123–146.

> Woods, P. (2002) 'Reintroducing creativity: Day 10 at Hackleton School.' *The Curriculum Journal*, Vol. 13(2), pp. 163–182.

> Jeffrey, B. (2003) 'Countering student instrumentalism: A creative response.' *British Educational Research Journal*, Vol. 29(4), pp. 489–504.

We are grateful to Taylor & Francis Books for permission to include an updated version of the following book chapter:

> Jeffrey, B. and Woods, P. (1997) 'The relevance of creative teaching: Pupils' views.' In Pollard, A., Thiessen, D. and Filer, A. (eds) *Children and Their Curriculum: The Perspectives of Primary and Elementary School Children*. London: Falmer, pp. 15–33.

We would also like to thank all the schools, teachers and young participants who have made this book possible.

We would like to thank our current colleagues Professor Geoff Troman and Professor Anna Craft for all their valuable assistance and collegiality covering the collection of this data and production of the various chapters in the past.

Introduction

Over the last half-century there have been two distinct stages in English primary education. The first, from the 1960s to the early 1980s, heavily influenced by the theories of Dewey (1929), Piaget (1973), Vygotsky (1964) and Bruner (1972, 1986), was dominated by a discourse of child-centredness, discovery learning and care. The second, from the mid-1980s to the end of the century, saw a complete contrast as education was given over to a discourse based on market principles, rational-technicism and managerialism, which squeezed the life out of creativity in many schools. We might now be entering a third stage, where creativity is making a reappearance but still within the structure and discourse of the second stage.

A certain amount of research has already been done on creative teaching but teaching is hardly creative unless it results in creative learning. This is to be our emphasis in this book. In this Introduction we set the scene by giving a brief review of creative teaching as it has appeared in our previous research, the onset of the stage of constraint from the mid-1980s, and the reappearance of creativity in policy and practice in recent years.

Creative teaching

In our early work on creative teaching we were impressed by the sheer *inventiveness* of primary teachers (Woods 1990). Their basic task was to find 'ways through' to pupil learning, and the nature of the task at times was something akin to detective work.

Once that was achieved, the aim was to maximise learning. Thus, schemes of work designed to be teacher-proof, like reading schemes, were used in creative ways, for example as subject matter for drama, advancing internalisation of the reading ability. But creativity was not just important for the pupils. It was essential for teachers' own 'self-renewal' (Woods 1995).

Creative teaching involves *ownership* of knowledge. The teacher is not simply relaying somebody else's information on to pupils, the conveyer of other people's news, which is then tested by instruments devised by others. The knowledge that they are concerned to produce and construct in children has been incorporated into their own life-worlds. It has become part of their own knowledge as applied to the social circumstances of their own classrooms and the social backgrounds of their students.

It follows that creative teachers have *control* of their own pedagogy. They choose what methods, and what combination of methods, to employ, and when. Creative teachers are also able to create and avail themselves of opportunities to teach creatively. They know how to exploit the 'implementation gap' between government educational policy and putting it into practice (Ball and Bowe 1992). They are also expert in taking advantage of the unexpected to promote learning.

None of this would be of any educational use unless the teaching was *relevant* to the child concerned – for the child to engage in creative learning, to make the knowledge his/her own and for it to become 'personal knowledge' (Woods and Jeffrey 1996, p. 116), to control learning processes, and for the learning to be innovative, to make a difference to the child. So often 'relevance' is defined by others in terms of what *they* perceive as pupils' and society's needs.

Creative teachers are concerned with 'person-making' (Brehony 1992), which involves the personal, social, emotional and intellectual development of children, 'teaching people to be people' (Woods and Jeffrey 1996, p. 57). It is about communicating, relating, mutual respect, working together, emotional well-being, knowing oneself and knowing others.

Creative teachers are passionate about their work. They care, strongly, about their pupils, in the way Noddings (1992) and Elbaz (1992) have described. Teaching is a moral craft (Tom 1984), about making better persons, and there can be no half-measures about that; nor can there be in teachers' commitment to their jobs. They are strongly vocational. They teach because they believe in it, not just for instrumental reasons. Teaching is part of their core identity, not something that can be separated from real selves (Nias 1989). They are enthusiastic, energetic, inspired.

In earlier work, we identified a wide range of creative teaching strategies, including: starting from the child; making home and school links; allowing children to revisit activities and thus develop their conceptual skills; 'teaching in the margins'; spontaneous reaction 'going with the flow'; making emotional connections; creating atmosphere and tone; stimulating the imagination; developing empathy; devising 'critical events' – akin to the projects of the Plowden era of the 1970s (Woods and Jeffrey 1996; Woods *et al.* 1999). These are just some of the strategies employed. They provide the flavour of everyday creative classroom teaching.

The growth of constraint

Global forces and the growth of the 'New Right' in government during the 1980s brought an end to the welfarist, humanistic, child-centred discourse that had prevailed since the 1970s, and in which creative teaching had flourished. Creative teaching was not simply replaced – it was derided.

Britain would lose out in the world if educational standards did not rise. The way to do it was through market forces, with schools competing for students and resources. League tables, drawn up by schools' performances on standardised national tests, would reveal the good and the not so good, and guide parents on where to send their children. Schools would earn their resources by numbers of pupils recruited. This emphasis on marketability and 'performativity' (an ideology of 'performance' with fixed goals, task analysis and testing, and the exclusion of any alternative view; see Ball 1998) dominated government policy. There was much more prescription in teaching, including a prescribed National Curriculum and less independent professional judgement. Ownership and control were wrested from teachers and assumed by the central government.

Values of care and creativity were squeezed out in the new instrumentalism and the all-consuming drive for higher standards – as measured by standard-ised objective tests. Managerialism replaced collegiality. 'Heavy-duty accountability' (Woods and Jeffrey 1996, p. 43) replaced professionalism and trust. Teachers' work intensified as all their spare moments at school and much of their home lives were taken over by new lesson preparation, form-filling, reports, and struggling to keep up with the pace of change during the 1990s (Hargreaves 1994; Woods *et al.* 1997). Teachers' creative abilities were now addressed to coping and survival rather than to teaching.

Primary education was now marked by two competing discourses – 'per-formativity', as championed by the government, and 'creativity', as espoused by many primary teachers – with widely contrasting values. One decreed a prescribed, controlled, subject-based curriculum; the other pre-ferred a negotiated, flexible, holistic one. One wanted a transmissional, behaviourist, formal pedagogy; the other a creative, constructivist, informal one. The government established formal, quantitative, standardised assess-ment; teachers would have preferred informal, qualitative, continuous assessment. Finally, performativity fostered a culture of competition, blame, managerialism and central control; teachers felt that a culture of collegial-ity, support, professionalism and self-regulation was more conducive to good education as they saw it (Jeffrey and Woods 1998). These polar oppo-sites clashed head on in the Ofsted school inspections of the 1990s, causing strong, disruptive feelings among primary school teachers, and signalling the onset of a rapid escalation of teacher stress (Troman and Woods 2001). There was a breakdown of trust between teachers and government, an increase of bullying of staff by head teachers, an increase in negative emo-tions – fear, anger, shame, guilt, anxiety, confusion – coping replacing creative strategies, and loss of professional identities.

Even in the gloomiest depths of the 1990s, however, creativity did not altogether expire (Woods 1995; Jeffrey and Woods 2003). Once teachers had overcome the first shocks, they showed their creative skills in adapting. As noted earlier, creative teachers are good at *appropriating* government policy so that it harmonises, or at least does not clash, with their own values and beliefs. One such attempt by a school we researched in the 1990s to appropriate the prescribed National Curriculum (which is based in part on principles of which the teachers disapproved, such as the compartmentalisation of subjects as against their holism) involved teachers:

1   recognising the threat of alienation that full compliance to the National Curriculum might entail;
2   sharpening their own beliefs through being forced to think about and articulate their philosophies;
3   engaging with the National Curriculum 'as a baseline from which to grow, not to become slaves to it, but actually to use it and adapt it in the ways that suit our philosophy and don't perhaps narrow our outlook too much' (Woods 1995, p. 72);
4   seeking alliances – with parents, governors, local inspectors, etc. – to seek to legitimate the appropriation. It will be seen here that there is a strong micro-political consciousness to this kind of teaching, necessary to gain and defend ownership. This school has found a way, it seems, of reconciling two apparently opposing discourses.

Towards the end of the 1990s and during the early 2000s, teachers such as these were to receive support from an unlikely source – the government.

The return of creativity

At the same time as the performativity discourse established its dominance in education early on in this decade, an international discourse of creativity (Jeffrey and Craft 2001) began to gain ground in economic, industrial, government and educational arenas. Its message was that creativity is eminently suited to the multiple needs of life in a new century, promoting as it does skills of adaptation, flexibility, initiative, and the ability to use knowledge on a different scale than had been realised hitherto (Seltzer and Bentley 1999). The government eventually came to realise that creativity was important both for individuals and for the nation in the rapidly developing, globalised world of the twenty-first century; and that it was not well served in the system they had set up. A number of government or government-sponsored reports and activities on creativity began to appear.

The Robinson Report (NACCCE 1999)

This noted that, while many teachers observed that their creativity was being squeezed by the literacy hour:

> There are schools and teachers who have used the literacy hour as a starting point for a wide range of creative activities in reading, writing, drama and in the other arts. We see great value in integrating the objectives of

high standards of literacy with those of high standards of creative achievement and cultural experience ... It would be of great value to many schools to have access to materials, ideas and strategies in the imaginative implementation of these strategies.

(NACCCE 1999, p. 79)

However, they felt that creativity did not go far enough in the new order, and recommended that 'creative and cultural education should be explicitly recognised and provided for in the curriculum, in pupil assessment and in school inspection' (ibid., p. 115). The report was welcomed by the then Secretary of State for Education, David Blunkett, who agreed that pupils should not only be equipped with basic skills, but 'should also have opportunities to develop their own potential'. His successor (Estelle Morris) talked of 'wanting to free the energies, talents and creativity of heads, governors and teachers to support them to achieve higher standards and to enable them to innovate and move towards earned autonomy' (Morris 2001, p. 6).

QCA Project on Creativity across the Curriculum (April 2000–4)

This was a three-year project to provide the Secretaries of State for Education and Skills and Culture, Media and Sport with advice on the potential for promoting pupils' creativity through the National Curriculum and to provide teachers with guidance on how they might do this. On the basis of their research the Qualifications and Curriculum Authority (QCA) developed a pack of materials designed to support teachers in promoting their pupils' creativity. The pack, entitled *Creativity: Find it, Promote it* (QCA 2003), is available on the QCA's website (http://curriculum.qca.org.uk), and seems to have been widely consulted. The QCA (2005) subsequently developed a video to accompany the materials and to give a clearer picture of various kinds of creative teaching and learning at various levels. The Secretary of State expressed his approval of these developments and of their continuance.

Creative Partnerships (Arts Council England) (2001)

Funded by the Department for Culture, Media and Sport (£110 million in 2002–6), this project aims to enable children in selected areas to gain creative skills through partnerships between schools and cultural organisations. By 2008 they had worked with over 2,400 schools in deprived areas. Ofsted reported that they had seen evidence of significant improvements in the basic learning skills of young people who had participated in Creative Partnerships activities (Ofsted 2006). There are examples of over 1,000 projects on their website (www.creative-partnerships.com/projects) and one of the projects upon which we report (Chapter 7) was funded by Creative Partnerships. Some examples are: in Cornwall, 'Trail of Giants', which matches artists and sculptors to create playgrounds, and 'Hole in the Hall', which involves a local poet and infant schools.

Between April 2004 and March 2005, 50 advanced skills teachers undertook a Creative Partnership experiential programme, exploring and developing their understanding of the theory and practice of creativity.

Report of the Joint DfES/DCMS Creativity Seminar for LEAs (DfES 2003b)

This report focuses on the progress of creative partnerships in some areas and of Local Education Authority (LEA) progress in getting creativity back on the agenda. Worcestershire, for example, claimed that they were overcoming teachers' fears and reluctance (after years of being pressed into uncreative teaching). Their

> strong focus has given schools the legitimacy to make creativity an integral part of the curriculum. The Department of Education (DoE) meets heads every term and bangs the drum for creativity – this has helped to legitimise a culture of greater risk taking in schools – though it has taken several years for schools to really begin to get this message.
>
> (DfES 2003b, p. 10)

They seek to move from the 'arts' towards 'broadening perspectives', which means embedding creativity in the whole curriculum.

There is an 'Artists in Schools' programme in three LEAs which encourages projects, continuing professional development for teachers (CPD), 'allowing them to explore what creativity is'. Models included arts centres and arts projects involving a mixture of private and public funding; others were totally LEA funded. Networks for creativity were important in promoting sustainability – between schools, between schools and creative organisations, and between LEAs and communities. DfES stressed the need for a statutory dimension on creativity to empower LEAs; and 'Government should do more to gather evidence of the benefits of creativity in education' (ibid.).

Nurturing Creativity in Young People (DCMS/DfES) (2006)

Joint action from these two departments following the NACCCE report and these seminars resulted in a new report entitled *Nurturing Creativity in Young People* (Roberts 2006). This wide-ranging document brings together economic, social and educational policies. Creativity is seen as a central component to establish 'creative portfolios for jobs' (p. 7). The report says that 'creativity is at the heart of personal, educational and career development' (p. 12) and there needs to be an 'overlap between creativity and independence, effective learning and critical themes' (p. 12) and an imperative to lead creative learning with teachers serving creativity more effectively (ibid., p. 20).

Excellence and Enjoyment: A Strategy for Primary
Schools (DfES 2003a)

One of the main messages for schools in this document is their need to focus
more on strategic learning: on thinking skills, creativity, reflection and
assessment for learning, study skills and collaborative learning. There's an
acknowledgement here of meta-learning and a flavour of constructivist
learning theory (though without acknowledgement) which had been
strongly criticised in the early 1990s. A set of CPD resources was prepared
by the Primary Strategy Team, *Learning and Teaching in the Primary Years*.
It has three key themes:

- Planning and assessment for learning
- Creating a learning culture
- Understanding how learning develops.

The resources can be used flexibly by schools to meet their individual
improvement needs as they see fit.

In his introductory speech accepting the Primary National Strategy
(PNS) Stephen Twigg, Minister of Education at the time, talked of creative
organisation, creative and cultural aspects, creative talents, creative thinking, creative partnerships, and creativity in learning, but only mentioned
performance in literacy and numeracy once, arguing that the latter were not
the 'be all and end all' of education.

Expecting the Unexpected: Developing Creativity in Primary
and Secondary Schools (Ofsted 2003a)

Some LEAs and schools may be struggling to get creativity inserted into their
Educational Development Plans (EDPs) or curricula. There are reports that
'schools still feel timid about developing a cultural and creative curriculum –
teachers continually ask if promoting creativity in schools will be acceptable
to Ofsted' (DfES 2003a, p. 11). But Ofsted has produced its own legitimacy.

This report is based on a small-scale survey by a group of Her Majesty's
Inspectors aimed at identifying good practice in the promotion of creativity
in schools. There is acknowledgement of some key aspects of creativity in
the report, but it retains Ofsted's distinctively stylised mode of reporting.
Thus, in the schools they studied, creative teaching is 'satisfactory' (less
than 10 per cent), 'good' or 'exceptionally good' (20 per cent).

This is still an enormous advance. And they take their lead from the
Robinson Report (NACCCE 1999). Creativity is 'imaginative activity fashioned so as to produce outcomes that are both original and of value'
(NACCCE, para 26, p. 29). Ofsted (para 7) states that 'the creativity
observed in children is not associated with a radical new pedagogy' (DfES
2003a, para 7, p. 5). It's more of a pragmatic thing. So they are not going

the full way to acknowledging that what we could be seeing is a recon-structed progressivism (Sugrue 1997).

National Teacher Research Panel (1999–)

Alongside these major reports and programmes the government has commis-sioned the National Teacher Research Panel set up in 1999 by its then sponsors, the Teacher Training Agency (TTA) and the Department for Education and Skills (DfES). Its initial purpose was to provide an expert teacher perspective to researchers, funders and policymakers on research pri-orities, projects and reports. Since then they have produced a range of research reports including 'Redesigning the curriculum to develop children's creativity', 'Developing a creative culture', 'Creative science', 'Can creativity projects improve the language and literacy skills of our pupils?' and 'Creative thinking in a community of enquiry' (www.standards.dfes.gov.uk/ntrp).

We can conclude from all this that creative teaching and learning are firmly on the official agenda and no longer outcasts. However, although there is official support for a creativity discourse and policies implementing some of its aspects, we have to ask: what kind of 'creativity' is envisaged? For what, and for whose purposes? Warning notes have been sounded by, amongst others, Hartley (2003), who argues that this new emphasis is func-tional for the economy. Creative teaching will produce consumers who are emotionally aware and creative in their quests to construct an identity. In other words, 'the expressive seems set to be managed for instrumental pur-poses' (ibid., p. 6). Ted Wragg (2004) suggested that once results from tests had flattened out, the government began putting the onus for raising stan-dards back on to teachers. They are still standards as perceived within a performativity discourse (Ball 2003). Elsewhere Wragg (2005) points to the stranglehold of controls the government has over education and shows no sign of relaxing, and asks, 'If "creative teaching" really is the government's aim for the future, how can schools shake off the suffocating embrace of nationalism?' (p. 5). Craft (2003) has brought to attention a number of prob-lems with regard to the fostering of creativity in education, such as difficulties of terminology, conflicts between policy and practice, limitations in curricu-lum organisation, limitations stemming from a centrally controlled pedagogy, and social, environmental and ethical specificity (p. 124). Alexander (2004) has mounted a powerful critique of the government's primary strategy, find-ing it 'ambiguous and possibly dishonest, stylistically demeaning, conceptually weak, evidentially inadequate and culpably ignorant of recent educational history' (p. 7). We still have no coherent and principled pedagogy (for which we now have an ample basis); rather a pseudo-pedagogy of prag-matism and compliance (pp. 28–29).

More recently it has been announced that the government is planning a new curriculum for the primary school to be implanted in 2010. The plan-ning group will be led by Jim Rose, one of the three authors of the 1992

Chapters 2–4 derive from research largely carried out between 2004 and 2006. Chapter 2 shows how, when teaching and learning is relevant to young participants, they take control of their learning. The chapter describes the way how, when teachers scaffold their teaching, learners eventually come to stand on their own feet. This involves various stages, including familiarising themselves with artefacts, phenomena or processes; taking over investigations in a mediating phase; and finally, moulding and crafting their learning.

Chapter 3 looks at the way in which the results of this developmental stage become owned by the learner. Ownership of knowledge is symbolised by the meaningfulness it has for the learner. It becomes part of their self and identity. Identity is seen to be a 'becoming' process as pupils play with their identities, value achievement and develop a sense of place about the context in which their investigations and learning occur. Ownership of their learning and subsequent knowledge is described through their interactions with knowledge, people and place. A social aspect is a major factor in our conceptualisation of creative learning and early in the chapter we provide examples of how three types of participative engagement framed their creative learning: co-participation, collective engagement and collaboration.

Chapter 4 focuses on what results from creative teaching that is new for the learner and how the learner is changed as a consequence. Relevance, control and ownership lead to innovations in the way knowledge is encountered, manipulated, understood and appreciated. It also leads to the development of the learner's acquisition of knowledge, the skills necessary to engage with knowledge and learning and a development of the person. This chapter provides examples of these innovatory experiences.

Chapter 5 begins Part II and draws on two case studies from the early 1990s which are no longer generally available, but which we consider still highly relevant today and which illustrate the themes in Part I. Both case studies discuss breakthroughs and transformations in pupils' learning and the processes leading up to them. Prominent among the factors for achieving breakthroughs is the use of pupils themselves as 'critical others'. The chapter details how these breakthroughs occur across most of the curriculum subjects and the effects on personal development. The chapter uses two inter-school projects, one involving a special school and a local primary and a joint school journey, and the other a rural and inner city exchange between two primary schools. In both case studies the social aspects of learning are shown to be influential in developing critical students and breakthroughs in learning.

Chapter 6 provides a case study of a few teachers from an inner city school with a predominately Asian intake appropriating the performative discourse and the dominant National Curriculum, to reintroduce a creative approach in stifling times – countering student instrumentalism (Jeffrey 2003). The pre-eminence of performativity policies and processes of the 1990s led in many cases to mutual instrumentalism (Pollard *et al.* 2000) where both teachers and learners worked to satisfy both individual and school performance targets. This chapter discusses creative mediation of policy by primary teachers and the successful achievement of a high level of learner ownership and control. We conclude that the clarification of learning objectives with the learners and the reconstruction of learning contexts has had an effect in countering learner instrumentalism. These approaches were effective in developing learners' awareness of the learning process and enabled them to articulate perspectives concerning those processes.

Chapter 7 is based on the teachers' perspectives from two of the schools involved in the 2004–6 creative learning research. It shows the ways in which these schools set about developing creative learning galvanised by the spaces created by the developing creativity discourse. It describes the re-emergence of teachers' past creative values, and how they have been institutionalising critical events in the guise of specialist programmes and external partnerships to achieve these objectives.

Chapter 8 is a study of the career of one village school over an eight-year period. Hackleton set out in the late 1990s to escape from the shackles of performativity and become a creative school. They began by suspending part of the timetable in favour of creative activities. This strategy inspired teachers and learners and led to school policies encouraging more creative teaching and learning during other parts of the week. The school went on to achieve an Artsmark gold award, to reconstruct its curriculum into 'curriculum flows', and to establish a programme of personalised learning, all against a background of high and improving test results. In this way the school reintroduced creativity into the curriculum through a strategy that was approved of by Ofsted, being placed on their 'Particularly Successful Schools' list and becoming an 'Innovative Practice Partnership' (IPP) school.

Finally, in Chapter 9 we consider the conditions for creative learning and how it might fare in the future policy arena.

There are two stories in this book. One identifies a particular type of creative learning rooted within a social framework. The other tells of the re-emergence of creative teaching and learning, strong and ubiquitous, though still fighting for legitimate space after serious decline during a period dominated by a performativity discourse. This discourse is still with us. How these two fundamentally opposing discourses, both apparently officially approved, become resolved in policy and practice will be one of the fascinating issues of the next decade.

Part I
The nature of creative learning

Creative learning has the same characteristics as creative teaching – relevance, control, ownership and innovation:

- Relevance. This is learning that is 'operating within a broad range of accepted social values while being attuned to pupils' identities and cultures' (Jeffrey and Woods 1997, p. 15).
- Control of learning processes. The pupil is self-motivated, not governed by extrinsic factors or purely task-oriented exercises.
- Ownership of knowledge. The pupil learns for herself – not for the teacher, examiner or society. Creative learning is internalised, and makes a difference to the pupil's self.
- Innovation. Something new is created. A change has taken place: a new skill mastered, new insight gained, new understanding realised, new, meaningful knowledge acquired.

Considering the relationship among these criteria, we have concluded that

the higher the relevance of teaching to children's lives, worlds, cultures and interests, the more likelihood there is that pupils will have control of their own learning processes. Relevance aids identification, motivation, excitement and enthusiasm. Control, in turn, leads to ownership of the knowledge that results. If relevance, control and ownership apply, the greater the chance of creative learning resulting – something new is created, there is significant change or 'transformation' in the pupil – i.e. innovation.

(Woods 2002, p. 7)

1 The relevance of creative teaching

Chris Woodhead (1995), ex-HM Chief Inspector of Schools in England, criticised the belief that 'education must be relevant to the immediate needs and interests of pupils', and argued that 'Our school curriculum must provide young people with the knowledge and skills they need to function effectively in adult working life' – a kind of relevance to society and to their own later life-chances. We would not disagree with the second point but see the first as a means towards its achievement. Without it, Morrison (1989, p.6), for example, feels that the 'art of teaching is lost to a series of narrow skills', becoming 'the casualty in a bureaucratized view of education in which education is called into the service of wider political ends and ideologies'. We have seen in more recent years how that art has been marginalised in the pursuit of performance in standardised tests. Yet the debate has not been one-sided; Wragg (1995), for example, urging the continuation of topic work and local projects, and space and time for teacher and pupil choice (see also Armstrong 1992; Webb 1993; Dadds 1994; Jeffrey and Woods 2003).

Pupils themselves have a great deal to contribute to this debate. Pupil perspectives are important because pupils are not just receivers or consumers of knowledge, but constructors of shared meanings in a combined exercise with teachers (Rudduck *et al.* 2004; Fielding 2007). Quicke (1992) has pointed out that these meanings are an aspect of 'metacognition' – knowledge about learning processes, about strategies of learning, and about people who are involved with them, like teachers. We might include in this a host of factors, notably the emotional, which affect the whole character of the learning enterprise and pupil's disposition towards it (Elbaz 1992). If we are concerned to produce autonomous, critical and reflective learners, and to improve learning, we need to know what sense pupils are making of what is offered to them, and how they view and feel about the circumstances in which it is being offered. It might then be possible to improve the pupils' metacognitive knowledge, and the context in which it is constructed. Without doubt, the teacher is one of the keys, if not the key elements in the development of metacognition.

Consequently, there has been a growing level of research into pupils' perceptions of teachers and teaching (Lord and Jones 2006; MacBeath 2006;

Rudduck 2006). For pupils in general, in other countries as well as the UK, the most important attributes of 'good' teachers appear to be that they should be 'human', should be able to 'teach' and make you 'work', keep control and be 'fair' (see Woods 1990 for a summary of this work). However, even if a teacher successfully establishes all these conditions to the approval of pupils, it cannot be assumed that they make the same sense of lessons as the teachers. It is not always realised how recondite the teacher's lessons sometimes are, or what pupils understand by 'work' and 'learning'. Also, while pupil responses have been organised into categories, as above, there are issues with all of the categories, such as sensitivity, feelings and trust, which may be more important since they are generic. These issues may be related to creative teaching and learning.

Our concern, therefore, in this chapter is to expand on the notion of 'relevance'. In broad terms, this involves teaching that is relevant to pupils' interests and concerns. It also includes pupil recognition of and identification with such teaching, with a sense of togetherness with the teacher and an empathy with her methods. Teaching and learning is a joint project. Relevance also has an emotional component, reflected in the nature of the pupils' engagement with such teaching. All this might be contrasted with the public, commodity, alienated knowledge so often associated with 'traditional' institutionalised learning. So much of the National Curriculum, especially in its earlier formulations, despite some benefits, was of this kind with its problems of overload, restriction of local adaptations, and formal, instrumental assessment (Campbell 1993a, 1993b; Pollard *et al.* 1994).

We have identified three areas of teacher pedagogy that are especially significant for relevant learning: ensuring positive social relations, engaging interest and valuing contributions.

Ensuring positive social relations

Positive teacher–learner relationships are central to the development of creative learning. The quality of social interaction determines how individuals act in situations and how their identities are created. Interpretations of language utterances and gestures determine responses. People imagine that they share each other's responses, sharing and mutually imbuing them with meaning, their manifestations make behaviour social (Mead 1934). The way learners are treated by their teachers determines their reaction to learning itself and to any engagement with teachers and schools in the learning process.

Our research in the early 1990s exemplified the commitment of creative teachers to social relations:

I feel that children as human beings – their holistic development, their relationships with me and with each other – is, for me, the first and most crucial thing because their attitude to learning and their own development will be affected by it. If they don't trust any adults or are unable to relate to each other when you sit them down to work together, the whole way that they are treated will show in the atmosphere. You know what kind of citizens you are helping to encourage, to develop. So that is very crucial to me and very crucial to really what you can achieve, educationally, in the standard of the reading, the writing, all of it. How they are able to work, how inventive they are able to be. Whether it's going really against the grain of growth or with it, limiting or expanding.

(Erica, T-C)

Learners feel that such teachers have their interests at heart and value them as individuals:

Well, when she's not here, we miss her, because then we have to get all different teachers, we have to go to other classes and things get mucked up in the class and the day seems a bit longer when she's away. People don't behave properly when she's away. We enjoy ourselves when she's here because she makes things easier for us.

(Angela, Yr4-I)

The relationship with their teachers also needs to be an honest one in which learners are not patronised but taken seriously:

I think that if you do something wrong she never really lies. Some teachers lie. If they don't think it's very nice they say, 'Oh! That's brilliant!' And they just say that will have to do. But Theresa [their teacher], if you do something wrong, just says, 'OK, that's not very good, go and do it again.' She doesn't say it horribly, 'Oh, that's really stupid, go and do it again!'

(Madeline, Yr5-SL)

A teacher's commitment to her profession enhances the relationship, for it shows learners that they are being taken seriously:

Theresa, my teacher, likes doing time machines, maps and Tudor gardens; she does a lot of imaginative work like the Tudor gardens, a lot of finding out about different times, science and experimenting. She also tries out new things from books.

(Hera, Yr5-I)

Being 'good at organising school trips and involving people from outside the school, like puppeteers and sculptors' (Sam, Yr4-I), shows a teacher's commitment to engaging the interests of learners. They can do what is officially required of them, but can also act under their own initiative, which earns pupils' respect:

She can do serious projects which are part of the National Curriculum, but she also likes to set up her things which she'd do at the weekend which we were grateful for and you have a laugh with, like doing little paintings or little origami lessons or something like that which is really good, which she's not really supposed to do ... But she's got her own side. She doesn't follow like a dog on a lead. She's not forced to do anything. She's not forced to get special lessons from outside the school. She puts herself out for us.

(Carla, Yr4-I)

Developing social relations is also seen as a positive teaching attribute:

She [the teacher] talks to the whole group together and then we just tell her our ideas, and other people comment on them and suggest this and that and then we put it all together. She lets us talk about it more than other teachers. She lets us have our own conversations and arguments and then gets us back to the point. She lets us speak, she lets us vote although we're not eighteen ... She lets us breathe more. Most of all she listens, unlike other teachers who jump to conclusions.

(Georgina, Yr6-G)

Such teachers often model behaviour:

When we argue, people join in and everyone puts in an idea. Other people have ideas and different cultures. We learnt this from Marilyn [their teacher] because she made us sit with different people and we had to get on with them. It wasn't that we didn't like them, it was because we didn't know them. When we had arguments she talked to us and showed us we aren't the only ones in the class. She taught us how to do what she was doing, like talk to us and sort out our problems. Now when we break up we sit down and talk to each other. She also talks to the whole group together. We tell her our ideas and other people comment upon them. We discuss things. She gets her board out and says, 'Let's sort this out.'

(Katy, Yr5-G)

Berger and Luckmann (1976) argue that the child passes through two phases of socialisation – primary and secondary. Primary socialisation is an induction into society through the subjectivity of others, and internalisation in this general sense is the basis, first, for an understanding of one's fellow man and, second, for the apprehension of the world as a meaningful and social reality (ibid., p. 150). They claim that this primary socialisation takes place under circumstances that are highly charged emotionally and they suggest that there is good reason to believe that without such emotional attachment to significant others the learning process would be difficult if not impossible (ibid., p. 151). Emotional connections between teacher and learner are important in developing common knowledge, that contextual framework for educational activities where the business of 'scaffolding' can take place (Edwards and Mercer 1987, p. 161) (see Chapter 2).

Teaching thus has an emotional heart for both teachers and learners. It is

> imbued with 'creative unpredictability' and 'flows of energy' ... In desire is to be found the creativity and spontaneity that connects teachers emotionally ... to their children, their colleagues and their work. Such desires among particularly creative teachers are for fulfilment, intense achievement, senses of breakthrough, closeness to fellow humans, even love for them ... Without desire, teaching becomes arid and empty. It loses its meaning.
>
> (Hargreaves 1994, p. 22)

This does not mean that the use of emotion is completely undisciplined and unchannelled. It can enervate teachers and students alike, but is also a subject of development as well as a means of motivation and contextualisation. Students' emotional development through drama, through narrative and story, and through relationships, and the general ethos of classroom and school, is a matter of prime concern. Teachers consciously attend to children's feelings in relation to learning situations and recognise emotional reactions as signals to be interpreted through the use of strategies such as a 'non-fault syndrome' and 'unblocking' (Woods and Jeffrey 1996, pp. 61–62) which act to involve learners rather than alienating them.

Many of these teachers are excellent performers and they create a variety of atmospheres which are related to the emotions (Woods and Jeffrey 1996). Humour 'brings more atmosphere to the class because if it was really strict it'd be a totally different atmosphere' (Carla, Yr6-I) but an abiding interest in learner welfare is also highly prized as relevant by learners:

> She gets excited when someone with a bad attitude problem comes on very well. When he's on report or something she comes along and supports him. She listens to people and their problems ... She's good at dealing with depressed people. She'll say 'excuse me, are you depressed about something?', then she'd relax you and talk to you personally. She'd just comfort you really ... She enjoys people sitting down in circles and people talking about this and that and the other, about different feelings they have.
>
> (Carla, Yr4-I)

Primary pupils are concerned about how to create and maintain feelings of confidence and they recognise many ways in which these teachers managed to do this. 'I would not shout at them for that would make them angry and would make it worse. I would help them with spellings for when I have to correct my work I feel scared that I'll get it wrong. I would whisper answers like Grace does ... She compliments us' (Tosin, Yr3-I).

Empathising is appreciated: 'When we're angry, she knows how it feels and she makes us feel better and solves the problem, helps us. She takes it easy on us. She has told us stories of her being angry when she was young' (Ishea, Yr3-SL). Pupils are keen to develop the relationship: 'We want to make Grace [their teacher] happy' (Toxs, Yr3-SL).

Getting things wrong is a worry for pupils and a supportive approach is also much appreciated:

> When you get a piece of work wrong she doesn't say, 'No, that's horrible, go and do it again.' She kind of explains it in a silly way that will make you go and do it again. She's quite funny when she speaks in a silly way. She puts her hands on her hips and kind of pretends to be angry but she really is joking. She does make us do it again, but she is not furious.
>
> (Tom, Yr5-SL)

Respecting pupils and valuing their opinions is important:

> Lee said, 'Why don't we let Georgina or Milton read the poem because they know Jamaica and they're black.' I said, 'Why? Because white people can read black poems too, just as I can read white poems.' Marilyn said, 'All right let's discuss it', and I read it and Lee read it. We all had a go. Some teachers might have said to me, 'Don't be rude.' She tells us calmly, she's always calm in our discussions.
>
> (Georgina, Yr5-G)

Engaging interest

The term 'fun' is often used by learners to describe teaching that stirs their interest: 'Because just listening and repeating is just boring. They want you to learn about the Tudors but they also want you to have fun. People say it's the best way to get something into your minds is to have fun' (Zizzi, Yr5-T). Fun is a 'catch-all' phrase used by pupils and teachers alike (Jeffrey and Woods 1997) to indicate depth of involvement and emotional connections:

> We made these treasure maps. Theresa [their teacher] didn't really tell us what to do. She just told us to make a grid and then make a treasure map, and we had to have instructions to find the treasure. They had to be really hard. We had to do the instructions on our own but we told each other things like, 'Hey! Look at that! That's great!' And sometimes we took ideas from other people if we couldn't decide what to do. I thought it was fun. We did homework on it as well, so we worked on it quite a lot. It wasn't like something which I'd look at and think, 'Oh no! We've gotta do the treasure map! I wish I wasn't in school today.' It was really exciting.
>
> (Hera, Yr5-I)

Relevance is increased if a real event is involved, one that is seen to be purposeful and worthwhile:

> When we were doing the cardboard seat for the playground I really did feel quite grown-up because we had a deadline and you had to say what it was going to be built out of. All the hard work paid off. It was really fun to think that it's my chair here in the playground, the one I designed. It was fun designing it and making it out of cardboard and wood and painting it and being able to actually help with the final construction. It's actually fun.
>
> (Usha, Yr5-T)

Pupil choice is also important:

> 'And it's our playground and we should choose some of the things we want for our playground. So when you go out into the playground you can think this was part of something you helped to make' (Emma). 'So, we don't feel left out' (Didea). 'I think they want us to be more involved round the school and here the things are mostly the children's choices so when it's finished it's what we want, not somebody else's choice' (Abdul).
>
> (Yr5-T)

This kind of teaching blurs the distinction between play and work:

> I visited a reception class (aged 5), and we discussed whether drawing was work or play or whether work was something the teacher asked them to do or whether play was better than work. I made the problem more difficult by pointing to examples in the room and asking if they thought the learners were playing or working, for example, one group were making paper daffodils. They argued with one another and changed their minds and provided other possibilities, but they now concluded that 'playing is fun but so is working sometimes'.
>
> (FN-17/03/03-S)

Being creative often comes naturally but the appropriate climate needs to be developed: 'I always do something different to everyone else. I have liked making things today because it was exciting and made me happy and I like playing with people, talking to them and laughing a lot' (Frankie, Yr4-S).

Even revising for a science Standard Assessment Task, perhaps the epitome of performativity, was considered fun if the right kind of engagement was sought: 'I think science was made fun when we were doing mind maps. They showed us what we knew and what we've learned and it shows you a way to remember things and it makes it more fun to revise' (Naomi, Yr6-T). The merging of play and work is 'really fun and you would enjoy yourself, but it's quite serious and you have to use a lot of imagination' (Nicholas, Yr5-H).

Fun does not mean that learning is an easy option. Learners find challenges, in the right context, enjoyable and worthwhile. One of the challenges during a maths trail around different classes was to see how far the learners could get doubling numbers, without calculators. Daniel starts at 110 'because I like a challenge. It doesn't matter if I don't finish' (Yr5-S). In this case the finished product is neither a requirement nor a focus. The process itself is seen as enough of a challenge to engage learners. Daniel started where he wanted to and determined the success criteria. The educational aim is to encourage his commitment to learning. Being challenged is a central element in building confidence but the context, the process and the pace of development was carefully planned by the guide.

> The dance teacher reminds them about the 'squashing the bug movement' and they focus on their leadership as they learn it and then at the floor with intense concentration. They are asked to pretend they are foot painting and one boy emphasises his 'cut' with his lips. They listen to instructions with fingers in mouths, hands over heads, stretching limbs and arms folded. They split into two groups and have to carry out the sequence a little after the first group begins. It is difficult but a challenge.
>
> (FN-5/02/04-H)

Intellectual rigour is welcomed in these circumstances and leads to meaning:

> It's a challenge. You have to keep at it. It's something you have to finish in the time available. You have to think about it and concentrate on it. When you finish it you have learnt something and achieved your goal and when you come back to it again you know what it means.
>
> (Jordan, Yr6-S)

It also brings a sense of joy in the achievement:

> A group are working on a maths problem focusing on Pascal's triangle in which the sum of the numbers at the end of each line of the developing triangle adds up to what are known as the triangular numbers, e.g. 1+2=3, 1+2+3=6, 1+2+3+4=10 etc. 'It's fun adding up and finding patterns between numbers. It's good finding a pattern in the position of the numbers. It's a finished piece, a masterpiece' (Seb).
>
> (FN-20/05/03-S)

These intense engagements, such as the drama sessions on Faustus, transform their learning experience as work and play merge into authentic labour:

> I enjoy it because it feels like it makes me excited and I want to read more of it and do more plays and learn more about it, like how it feels to be Dr. Faustus. If I was reading a book and it was interesting I might

do a play about it and then you can create anything you want. It makes you want to write about it and to do a story setting, something different, but not exactly the same. It just makes you interested about it and just makes you creative.

(Anton, Yr5-T)

Similarly, physical rigour is exacting but satisfying:

In the introduction they stretch to the music up and over and smile and laugh as their arms go in different directions. They perform a canon movement following the last person round the circle. Each person then decides on a movement and they all have to copy it. These are all very innovative and the children seem to enjoy them. They then do their standing still sequence to music with the teacher at the front of the hall. All concentrate, trying hard and extending every movement to its fullest extent with slight smiles indicating their increasing confidence but with their eyes still on the teacher and they are very still at the end.

(FN-9/03/04-H)

Andrew (Yr6-G) loved his role playing in a play in Tudor times:

What was I enjoying about being there? Oh, that's a tricky one. Well I think it was making the audience laugh. I was being tortured, but when I stretched my legs out and everyone started laughing I thought, 'Please don't make myself laugh, please, please!' I made it even funnier, but I was saying to myself, 'I mustn't laugh', and I just kept my laugh in.

The overcoming of fear and anxiety can also be fun, for young participants often test the boundaries and parameters of their environment:

'I like the fact that we went to the Albany theatre to present our play of the Faustus Tudor project but it was quite scary standing up in front of people and doing it' (Sophie). 'I coped with the fear by squeezing my hand into a fist so I wouldn't be scared. Your nerves are wracking, even though we have been doing it for a few months. Even if the teacher said I didn't have to do it if I was scared I'd still vote for doing it' (Anton). 'Your heart is beating really fast 'cos you are so nervous' (Abdul).

(Yr5-T)

Risk taking is also a major part of the exploratory adventure that is fun. For early learners, gaining control depends on opportunities to play with ideas and to be allowed the time for sustained energy, sometimes realised in good home–school relations. However, routines also enabled control to escalate as learners gained the confidence to take risks (Woods *et al.* 1999). Young people experiment from an early age and young learners often want to continue to push boundaries at the same time as they become more aware of the consequences of taking risks.

> They then take a partner, who has their eyes closed, on a journey in this scientific investigation of blindness in their history project. They were encouraged to use different levels. They must trust the leader who will only use her hand to indicate the direction. Kate asks them what made it eird. They tell her that 'they wanted to keep their eyes open', 'that they were afraid they couldn't trust the person', 'they had a map in their head, but I worried that I would crash into someone', 'I could hear people coming closer but my partner turned me away', 'I became confused and dizzy going up and down'.
>
> (FN-19/01/04-T)

Peer social relations are as important to young participants as those with teachers: 'It's fun and it's good to be co-operative and you can talk to each other and you can make things, share ideas, put them together and then something good might happen so it's good to share ideas' (Imogen, Yr5-V). The joy of working together helps make the activity relevant, as in this case of exploring the Beginning of the World project through dance:

> Some pairs focus on each other as they construct a 'big bang' for the world's beginning. Another pair survey the room and discuss the composition by a pair of boys. One girl moves a partner into position to match the music. The girls talk about their movements together and the boys demonstrate and someone else claps them. The pairs demonstrate a composition and two girls keep up the pace and the rhythm of the maracas that the teacher is playing. They fall to a scissors shape together with a turn, a roll and a jump. Another pair face each other and march towards each other in a confrontational scissor battle.
>
> (FN-17/10/03-Yr5-V)

The use of role playing for pupils is also recognised as important and valuable by pupils, supporting Paley's (1986, p. 128) observation that 'School begins to make sense to the children when they pretend it is something else'.

> You get to be different people and you can act out the events. It's enjoyable because you can just go along with it, and it's the way you do it that makes you enjoy it ... I like being other people. There's all the parents there and everybody else and me being all these characters. I like having loads of parts.
>
> (Nicola, Y6-G)

Drama is 'a good way how to learn history' (Nicola, Yr6-G). 'You can't actually remember all the dates but if they make it like fun, like this, it's easier'

(Nicola, Yr6-G). It's 'easy to have fun and when you're learning you think it's easy. Some bits might not be so easy but then again you're still having fun. Fun makes you think it is easy and when it gets difficult you go on because it is fun' (Osha, Yr5-T). These wise words from a 10-year-old show us how teachers make learning relevant to young participants through engaging their interest and making learning enjoyable and meaningful.

Valuing contributions

Young participants come to school with opinions (Pollard 1987), beliefs, perspectives, reflections and reflexive accounts. They are able to join in discussions, negotiations and evaluations. An appreciation of these qualities and the opportunity to express their views, values, questions and understandings enhances relevance. If they are allowed to contribute they will experience learning as an open and challenging experience; if not they will witness learning as conforming and develop an increasingly dependent relationship on school adults (Pollard *et al.* 2000). Pupils have the capacity to become connoisseurs of learning, and to be active, knowledgeable contributors.

Learning connoisseurs

Our research showed many examples of this connoisseurship, particularly in assessing and evaluating curriculum programmes and pedagogy. 'I would break it up a bit sometimes. I would make them work by themselves to become independent. I would also like them to use their own ideas as well as using other people's ideas. But I would also like them to be able to work with other people' (Lottie, Yr6-T). As they crafted their learning experience and worked to make it meaningful they built up knowledge of teaching and learning. They learnt how to analyse and evaluate it. They were going through a process of becoming experienced learners: 'Instead of sticking to one thing you're trying different things, you're opening your mind, being more creative' (Abdul, Yr6-T).

Young participants understood the relationship between learning and achievement. They spoke of subjects that they liked but in which they were not so competent: 'I like literacy because of the writing. I'm not good at science but I like the experiments; however, I struggle to understand it sometimes' (Sophie). 'I don't like writing stories. I like bike riding and football but I am not good at them' (David) (Yr4-S). They had knowledge of what it meant to be a consumer of education but due to their experience of creative learning this was not limited to instrumental teaching and learning. 'I think we like to learn different things. We've got different minds and we like to learn different things' (Mazie, Yr5-V).

They were sensitive to the necessity for curriculum and pedagogic balance (Lord and Jones 2006; Pollard *et al.* 2000):

It's good because it ain't the teacher telling you what to do; you're making up your own movements and dances. It gets kind of boring if the teacher is always telling you what to do. It makes you independent. It's good to make up your own dance although sometimes it's good for the teacher to tell you what to do. That can be fun too.

(Ronnie, Yr5-H)

They used their evaluations to make recommendations: 'I don't think the teacher should have had a go at her like that. I would have asked them why they had done it wrong and not just shouted at her straight away. The teacher didn't know whether she was hurt or something, when she appeared to be a little slow' (Will, Yr5-V). They were able to give advice as to how to transfer the experience of dance to other domains:

'You could use dance to show what it used to be like in olden times and how they felt, and how they used to dance, or you could compare theirs with modern dance' (Opie). 'You could show how they felt in school in the Victorian times or how they worked for money as an orphan. You would show them crowded in a corner and thinking about things that are going to happen later in life' (Sheera).

(Yr6-H)

The young participants used all their inventiveness to explain how to use dance in maths: 'You could pretend to be numbers and dance something like a sum. Someone could lie down on the floor; someone could curl his self or her self. Someone could be on top of someone. Somebody should be the add sign. And you would get more interested in the subject' (Jordon, Yr5-V). And other areas of the curriculum:

This might sound a bit silly, but sometimes in literacy you could dance the stories and in geography you could be the plane going up and down or you could do the splash of water or a tidal wave or something. I think singing and dance could help you do the rhythm. You'd learn spelling through the shape of the letter – Mrs D, Mrs I.

(Gemma, Yr5-V)

They knew how learning could be more effective: 'The dance project helped because the teacher didn't actually show us the working of the planets through their movement but when we used dance we understood what the teacher was telling us about it. You remember because you think of the movements and you remember that the earth goes round slowly' (Victoria, Yr5-V). They used this knowledge to evaluate teaching strategies:

'The teacher shows us in a very slow way and if it looks like we're a bit confused then they do it again, and they make sure we get it right rather than just sitting there and doing nothing' (Lottie). 'I think the teacher is strict, which is good because when people are strict they get you to work faster and you get more into it' (Carl). 'What I like about the dance teacher is that they repeat things for about three seconds and then move on to something new' (Corin). 'What I like about the teacher is that they don't give up when people can't do it, either they go over there and help or they get someone who knows how to do it to help' (Mazie).

(Yr5-V)

They challenged stereotypes:

At the London Dungeons there's this bit of Henry VIII as a ghost. He's eating the chicken and going 'Burp!', and just throwing the chicken. It ain't real proof though is it? I'd prefer not to know a load of lies like different stories. I'd like to know the real thing that happened.

(Jamie, Yr6-G)

They understand the nature of situations such as Ofsted inspections: 'They were like ice people. Though sometimes they smiled, they didn't sound humorous, and they slid in and out like ghosts' (Aysha). 'Our teacher was different. She tried her best. She glared at us a lot rather than tell us off. She came round a lot and gave us clues, patted our heads and marked our work a lot. Annoyance came through her eyes and her smile' (Sheila). 'Some of the teachers got angry with us because they were tired with too much work to do. I saw our teacher with her head in her hands, and when I asked what the matter was, she said she was so tired. Our head teacher apologised to us later for shouting. He thought we were going to mess up the inspectors' room' (David) (Yr5-I). They are able to identify power shifts: 'She had power, but when the inspector came in they asked her questions, and when they left the power faded and when they returned so did the power' (Rachael, Yr6-SL).

Active contributor

Relevance encourages learners to contribute:

Last week the children composed a set of movements suggested by Avril – high, low, turn, etc. – modelling. After the class Nimra suggested to Avril, the dance teacher, that they come up with ideas for each other, so Avril included it this week. She asks the rest of the class to compose a sequence for a group of four in the centre of the hall. They suggest: 'go fast and high, show a turn, circle arms and legs, work in line clicking fingers, canon along the line'. The children clap the efforts. They suggest 'three go high and three low, push each over like dominoes in a canon, do a low-high split and then reverse it, all fall over, separate from one another, get into a row and finish sitting, make a letter p'.

(FN-9/03/08-Yr5-H)

Some teachers include a formal evaluation in their teaching programmes to make the whole process relevant and inclusive.

> Veronica (Sounds in the Environment project artist) and Andrea (class teacher, Yr4-S) carried out an evaluation with the children during the afternoon. They had to write down all the 'sound' project activities on pieces of paper. The children write lists of what they have learned. They have to pick three of the activities and order them according to how scary they are. They have to put all orange circles on the yellow strip in order from the most enjoyable to the least enjoyable sound activity. They then lay them out on their tables and walk round reviewing others' prioritisations. They are then asked how they would develop the project with one child in each group writing down the answers, e.g.: 'I would carry out a treasure hunt in the zoo' (Josh). They were asked whether they would prefer to work with an outside artist periodically as they have done once a week or blocked in a whole week. They were then asked if they had seen anything different about the way Andrea had worked and one reply was 'she was not a teacher all the time' (Josh, Yr4-T).
>
> (FN-1/12/03)

Very young participants contribute spontaneously and these may sometimes be critical evaluations.

> I go to one of Frank's (sculpture artist) workshops with Yr1. The children sit on logs in a square in an art room. In front of them is a large square piece of material and in the centre is a coloured circular design made up of brightly coloured pieces of material. They are invited to distribute pieces of calico and other materials around the central design. 'I know I'm going to put this here.' 'I put my one across your blue one.' 'You said we were going to do messy art. This isn't messy art; if we do a dodo will make it messy.' 'I put mine on yours.' 'This isn't very exciting.' 'Some of the colours have covered up the blue; it looks like an arrow [after selecting some pieces of wood that have been painted white]. It looks like a chicken drumstick, it looks like it's in the water.' 'We've done a cross for England.' 'Why are we doing this?' 'A line down the middle would be quite good, that looks nice.'
>
> (FN-4/02/04-T)

Including young participants in discussions about their practice also develops it as a 'learning to learn' approach. 'At the end of the IT session (with Yr4) the teacher asked them to indicate whether they thought they had extended themselves or helped someone. She then asked them whether they thought they had worked hard and achieved something and whether they wished to push themselves further. At the same time this particular teacher was open to use their expertise. On occasions the teacher was unable to find a particular button or tab that she required on the computer keyboard and she asked openly if any of the class could assist her in a general chatty manner. She told me later that she was aware that some of the children had used this programme at home and she publicly acknowledged their expertise, ensuring a co-participative relationship' (FN-17/03/03-S).

Their initiative even resulted in them leading the direction of classroom action:

> One boy said, 'I'd like to show what I mean in a model, could I do a model?' 'Yes please,' I said, 'do a model.' It was a fantastic three dimensional model which I couldn't have done and it inspired the other children, took them in different directions.
>
> (Tess, Yr5-T-S)

Teachers' willingness to put learners' enquiries at the centre of investigations ensures that learners see the relevance of their practice:

> One of the Foundation teachers says, 'Don't wear your jumper round your stomach. It looks untidy.' Amy, a child, chimes in with 'It might hurt your blood and bones. It might make your blood go up and up and up to your ear and explode like it did to my sister.' The teacher develops the situation quickly by asking, 'What is an explosion? Come and draw it on the board.' The drawing shows arms going up into the air.
>
> (FN-22/05/04-S)

In the hands of a skilled teacher and a real project, such as the construction of benches in a playground with the assistance of a project artist, learner contributions become part of the project evaluation itself:

> When we came to the model stage they were given free rein from their paper-based ideas, going on to the model making and Sam, the artist, led this brilliant session where they talked about the designs and what could be made with the materials we've got and all of a sudden we've got 9- and 10-year-olds saying 'this is unrealistic' or 'this would work really well'.
>
> (Graham, Yr5-T-T)

Encouraging active contributions engages enthusiasm and commitment:

> Kate, the drama teacher, has arrived and the class write a libretto to a tune some of the children had composed. Kate has added the backing and a harmony. The children listen to the music intently and then chatter and smile at the end and the composer explains his methodology: 'I spent time at playtime, made up the song and tried it out on the piano.'

Another adds to the libretto: 'Because we were studying Faustus and hell we thought we should have the phrase "guts hanging out" because that was what was going on in his head' (Leithan). Mickey suggests that they use the phrase 'rip their guts out' rather than 'pull their guts out' and this is agreed. It is agreed that the children will email Kate with further suggestions.

(FN-23/03/04-S)

Conclusion

Much that is here echoes the existing literature on pupil perspectives on 'good' teachers. It is perhaps unsurprising that pupils like teachers who are human, understanding, humorous, can explain, and make you work. But these pupils add a further gloss to this. By reflecting on their own reactions to these qualities, the pupils tell us something about their own metacognitive knowledge – about their knowledge of how they learn, and of shared understandings with teachers. But they also strongly suggest that creative teachers encourage creative learners. Looking at the pupils' comments we can see that these teachers' pedagogy is seen by pupils as having a direct bearing on their lives.

It is not enough, however, simply to be relevant. Relevance has to be demonstrated and achieved. Students have to know and feel the relevance themselves. Their comments here tell us how their teachers achieve this through developing social relations, emotional connections and engaging interest. In this, we might see some of the properties of what Claydon *et al.* (1994, p. 172) describe as 'authentic activity', involving 'putting the pupil into the engine room, as it were, of knowledge creation' (see also Bridges 1991). There are, further, elements of the 'socially critical primary school' as argued for by Morrison (1989), sustained by a form of progressivism based on 'creative thinking, self-awareness, and inner strength' (Zimiles 1987, p. 204). This involves a holistic view of pupils, viewing them as rational agents, but taking into account 'all their capacities – "emotion" and "will" as well as intellect' (Quicke and Winter 1993, p. 2).

2 Control of learning

The control of learning processes involves having a measure of self-direction over how one learns and having a range of choices, as opposed to being instructed to learn by the teacher in a certain way, through, for example, rote learning. Our data suggest that learner control of learning progresses through three phases: 1) familiarisation, 2) mediation and 3) moulding and crafting. In the first phase learners familiarise themselves with the context, the task and resources. In the second they mediate these mainly through the use of their imagination. In the final phase they mould and craft the construction of an outcome. These three attributes are examined in detail in the rest of this chapter.

Familiarisation: scaffolded engagement

The control learners gain is not total, unbounded or socially disengaged. It is limited by the learning context, influenced by teachers and peers and is dynamic, with learners having more or less of it during the process of engagement. It is not so much given by teachers or adults. Young participants have come from early childhood experiences where, in general, they felt very much in control of their world, investigating and owning a great deal of it (Winnicott 1964), albeit bounded by family supervision constraints, such as limitations on the distance travelled away from adults and limited access to harmful or inappropriate materials. Early years schooling generally recognises the effectiveness of encouraging young children's control over learning (Beetlestone 1998; Craft 2002) but later years of schooling often curtail their control in order to 'deliver' the curriculum. Creative teachers aim to reinvigorate children's interest in controlling their own learning and to ease any constraints placed upon learner actions.

A general strategy for this is 'scaffolding' (Bruner 1986) based on Vygotsky's 'zone of proximal development' (Vygotsky 1964) created by teachers and adults but mediated by young participants through language and social engagement. Children travel through the zone gradually gaining understanding of it through the support of the relevant adult and their use of imagination. Adult language is imbued with conceptualisations of knowledge and cultural histories and it acts as a scaffold for the learner to engage with new knowledge. In general terms, the teacher is an enabler and facilitator, aiding children to learn how to learn.

The Reggio schools provide one example of scaffolding in action. There, learning is based on opportunities to choose, to make mistakes, to choose where and with whom to invest curiosity, intelligence and emotions, to do this without anyone arbitrarily setting timing/rhythms, or measures. But Reggio teachers argue it cannot be left to chance: adults have to be involved. Creative teaching will only happen when children are assured of broad and active co-participation of adults (Emilia 1996, p. 36).

Learners need nourishing (Craft 2005) and opportunities to participate with teachers, significant others and peers (Cocklin *et al.* 1999), as well as time and space to engage with materials and ideas. The atmosphere or climate of a learning experience fuels the creative process, motivates activities, marshalling the physical and the mental to experiment, use predictions and cooperate over findings and hypotheses.

Scaffolding in creative learning is not facilitation but co-participation. Young participants in learning situations clamber all over the scaffold, familiarising themselves with the terrain, choosing their own direction, imagining new images and constructions from different junctions on the scaffold. They take risks as they leap from level to level and swing out into space and leap from bar to bar of the scaffold, eventually finding a place to construct their representation while remaining aware of the habitation of other spaces in the scaffolded structure by their peers whom they can observe and draw upon as they create their products, solve their problems or carry out investigations. The young participants in an environment of this sort work at different levels of the scaffold and move between them as and when it suits them, passing their peers and sometimes joining them.

Early guidance was appreciated in the dance project to develop Yr6 confidence as the participants were able to latch their bodies to the task and then develop it:

> I think they were a little bit more inhibited then. They really needed the guidance of the teacher as to how to creep along. Some of them were just walking through it; they weren't really putting themselves in the place. But that girl is really thinking about what the teacher is telling her to do, not just watching, whereas some of them, at the beginning, really needed the guidance to see him doing it first.
>
> (Doreen, Yr6-T-V)

From the participants' point of view the scaffolding was creative: 'They teach us and I make up my own movements, it's good when they say scrunch or leap, or things like that. This gives you guidelines and then you make it up yourself' (Franklin, Yr5-V). Creative learning has to be effective if it is to be incorporated into national pedagogies – effective in processing a national curriculum, effective in the learner gaining understanding and knowledge and effective in making learning experiences meaningful. Scaffolding by teachers and other significant others is a risk taking but secure context in which learners can take some form of control.

Maths is the one specific subject where some pupils feel they need teachers to be supportive, as Angela (Yr5-SL) explains:

> She's [the teacher] good at maths because she doesn't make it too hard for us. She does it the long way, and if you're not sure, if you don't know, then she gets you to sit on the mat and she'll help you. It keeps on going like that and we get the answers right.

It is significant that a number of children describe teachers as good at particular subjects when the teachers actively help them succeed at a task, rather than assessing teachers in terms of their depth of knowledge of the particular subject.

Some pupils also value the time they have to engage with their activities in depth. Yr6-G had been seen working on one drawing on and off for a couple of weeks: 'We need the time to do it in greater detail instead of in a rush. You can tell if something's been rushed or been done slowly' (Lee, Yr6-G). However, they appreciate high standards within the appropriate relationship: 'She doesn't let you off doing it because Richard had to write the invitation to the governors out eleven times until he got it right' (Tom, Yr5-SL). They appreciate both high standards and generosity:

> When she's talking to you she sort of understands you, and if you don't understand it, she doesn't give up like sometimes your mum and dad do. If you do work for them, they go, 'Oh! I give up!' But with Theresa, she carries on listening to you and carries on, even if it takes all day.
>
> (Madeline, Yr5-SL)

They also appreciate any respect given them: 'She expects us to use our brains' (Hera, Yr5-SL).

Teachers devise significant learning contexts such as special curriculum weeks where time becomes elastic for learning at a different pace: 'When you have a whole week the children who work at a slightly slower pace pick up more because they're able to repeat, re-visit in a larger chunk of time' (Clare, Yr2-T-S). They also take into account particular learning styles (Claxton 1999): 'We also make a point of looking at the ways in which children learn, some are kinaesthetic learners, some are audio learners, some are visual learners, and we try to build this in to our planning' (Clare, Yr2-T-S).

Teachers thus adapt to the fact that 'some children work in different ways. You've got to offer a range of teaching strategies. Children are individuals just as adults and it's up to us to offer a full range' (Sheila, T-S). They allow themselves time and space to be able to respond to a learner's enthusiasm and so build on their interest: 'We've just done journeys, for our geography project, which we've taken all over the place. Paddington Bear, who was off to Peru, just took off so we stayed with that. We always make sure we've got that flexibility; we never cut ourselves short on projects' (Jayne, F-T-S).

Creative teachers welcome a negotiated approach (Woods 1990): 'I think this is wonderful that we're looking at how we learn and how best children learn. It would be totally narrow minded of me to say this is the right way and this is the wrong way if the children will share with me how they got from A–B. I can always adapt that, change that, learn from that and act as a catalyst' (Tess, Yr5-S).

Teachers set up the context:

> We're doing the adventure playground so I'm thinking of different resources we can use, so I can demonstrate things to the children, e.g. how to fold straws, make cones. Children then take it on themselves and their creativity comes out more with individual styles of what they're actually doing. They find the basics and then go off and do their own thing. In that respect it affects their learning in a concentrated way.
>
> (David, Yr1-S)

They encourage scope and provide clear direction, 'I think we've broadened the children's education in terms of their own perception of how they can learn' (Clare, Yr2-S), but they still need guidance to take control: 'I think children in a primary school actually need to be given clear instructions and they need to be able to get their hands on and do it' (Vicky, HT-S).

Teachers take account of individual differences:

> Children of this age, especially, like to see something through. Some children come out with these bursts of creativity at the beginning. Then there are the ones who like to weigh things up and take a lot longer. So when you've got a concentrated period for doing it such as the curriculum weeks it helps everybody out. Some have got some idea at the beginning, then by the end of the week it's consolidated and some are just getting it by the end of the week.
>
> (Hen, F-T-S)

Control over their own learning processes may well be bounded by the task but this still provides opportunities for creative learning:

> We spent a whole day doing technology with work on bridges. I watched how they put the various skills together, maths and in different ways literacy and all the other skills – physics, dexterity. There was a whole learning experience, team building. They needed to work together, to identify which skills they were best at. They all had a go at rolling the paper tubes, skills at putting it together, focusing in on and they learnt

from each other, learnt to help each other. There was a certain amount of team building and identifying your own skills, they had to cooperate.

(Chris, Governor-S)

Scaffolding of this kind includes possibility thinking (Craft 2002), an attitude which refuses to be stumped by circumstances, but uses imagination, with intention, to find a way around a problem. It involves the posing of questions, whether or not these are actually conscious, formulated or voiced. It also involves problem finding. Being able to identify a question, a topic for investigation, a puzzle to explore, a possible new option, all involve 'finding' or 'identifying' a problem. It can be greatly aided by computers:

The computer suite consisted of three hexagonal workstations over a metre high with the children sitting on high chairs sharing a computer between two of them. It looked like the central control panel in Doctor Who's Tardis and the head teacher told me it had specifically been designed to be attractive to young learners. It was a light airy room with lots of computer designs and relevant vocabulary spread around the walls. The hexagonal design encouraged the children who sat round it to consult and collaborate with each other easily. The learners pressed their fingers to their lips as they gazed at the screens exhibiting puzzled brows, balancing on the edges of their stools as they slowly revolved them backwards and forwards. One hand covered the mouse with a constantly twitching forefinger stabbing at its shoulder and the other hand occasionally dabbed at the screen or searched for an appropriate button. They debated and evaluated choices, quality and techniques.

(FN-17/03/03-S)

The scaffolding process may take time to pass through the 'proximal plane of development' (Vygotsky 1978), a landscape in which learners build on their experience, knowledge and level of development with the assistance of the teacher and then gradually gain ownership of the subject matter. 'Giving lots of vocabulary in the warm up seemed to work, and they seemed more confident, much happier to show their work. I think a lot of that isn't necessarily anything I particularly did, but the fact that they knew more about what to expect' (Avril, Dance Teacher-H).

However, the process is not just a linear one. The arrival at the 'proximal plane of development' was sometimes almost simultaneous with the construction of the scaffold: 'When the teacher is talking we sit down while they tell us what to do. Me and my partner think while they're talking' (Katie). They 'take ideas from the teacher and turn it into something different' (Joe). Given the opportunity to be creative, as in this dance and confidence building project, the participants took it: 'The teacher tells you something and you have to get a picture in your mind and this one was a box and I got a picture in my mind of a chest, the way it opens and it slammed shut, so we made it with our bodies' (Franklin) (Yr5-H).

Mediating: taking off and taking over

This mediating phase involves learners gaining more confidence in handling materials and ideas and bringing their own experiences and imagination to the task. Having familiarised themselves with the materials and ideas, they move to incorporate them into their own sphere of control through exploration and playfulness. They begin to dismantle the scaffold and take over the direction of the activity, launching out on untrodden paths.

Creative learning involves imagination, invention and anticipation, the organisation and control of ideas and judgements (Halliwell 1993). The Reggio Emilia schools in Italy work with a pedagogy that cultivates a child's capacity to give the right shape to his or her life. But this capacity is only achieved if young participants exercise that right. These schools see young participants as born with the languages of life and as being interactive by nature, equipped with exploratory tools for organising information and sensations and for seeking out exchange and reciprocity:

> 'Being artistic means that your mind is running wild' (Daisy). 'I think that Creative Partnerships are making us creative because you have to think of opening your mind like the winner of the recent sculpture competition was a bowl of fruit in the playground for sitting on' (Lara).
>
> (Yr6-T)

They were full of ideas about how to develop expression and also keen to take control of the techniques and processes: 'Instead of being told lots of things that we are meant to do most of the things that you do come from your imagination really. It's like when you make things up, you can do anything you want' (Isabelle). 'It's not all them, them, them, you get a chance to do it' (Corin) (Yr5-V). However, imagination isn't without contexts or references:

> Cloe tries to make a 'spooky' picture – from play with a seven piece tangram that fits together to make a square – 'because the background picture is black. Does it look like a ghost? It's floating. It has a tail like some ghosts and these are the arms like wings helping them to fly. I'm going to do a spider. It's hanging from there. I decided to make it because you find them in spooky places.' James constructs a design and then used his imagination to determine its use. 'I have made a sign that goes on a baby changing door. It struck me straight away. It's my first choice and it looked real. It looks like a baby holder, like a clip.'
>
> (FN-19/05/03-Yr6-S)

Younger children use their imagination spontaneously as they encounter a creative situation in an art and design lesson:

The Year 1 children sit on logs in a square in an art room. In front of them is a large square piece of material and in the centre is a coloured circular design made up of brightly coloured pieces of material. This was constructed by the previous group. The children comment as they sit down and suggest: 'it is a large lump', 'it looks like a boiled egg', 'it looks like an eyeball', 'it looks like a baby sleeping', 'why don't you put yellow all around it?', 'you would need four people to do that', 'it might be a colourful egg', 'it looks like a beautiful rainbow', 'I think it's a giant lollipop', 'they are terrapins', 'they are flowers in a garden', 'this is a sea', 'that is an egg', 'this is a pond with a shell'.

(FN-4/02/04-T)

Taking over meant immersing oneself into the narrative of the specific investigation: 'The "Beginning of the World" project was like a journey because when we started it there were animals and darkness and you had to go round each other and it was all dark and you couldn't bump into each other and you had to go round each other and it reminded me a lot like of the earth and the sun' (Gemma, Yr6-V).

Learners being creative is crucial for creative teachers: 'Often the children come up with ideas and spark off your ideas so you can take it one stage further and it's that spontaneity which helps the creativity' (Brenda, Yr2-T-S). Their innovative mediating means 'children take it on themselves, creativity comes out more, individual styles of what they're actually doing, find the basics and then go off and do their own thing really, in that respect it affects their learning in a concentrated way' (David, Yr1-T-S).

Creative learners become immersed in playful engagement (Rogers 1970) during a design and technology activity involving computer and literacy skills:

The children have made a computer model of a classroom. They also have to write a text to explain each picture and what is exciting about it. They make no fuss or show any excitement on getting out their terminal and find their projects on the laptops with confidence. They select shapes and use the colour bar to fill in effects with ease. Hamish and Kuran tell me that 'it is a nature place, a reptile room with pods where the animals live. There are two Jacuzzis, one for the animals and one for the learners.' They construct 12 different coloured leather seats and there is a computer on each table. There is an animal table, a bath, a reptile pod, seats and a white board. There are two shelves going down the sides of the classroom. They feed the animals and 'study them and make them better if they are ill'. They were 'proud of their idea of making a reptile classroom. It was different to everyone else's and we chose a simple design.'

(FN-19/01/04-T)

The learners easily recognise the value of being allowed to engage playfully: 'Because they picked our ideas not their ideas, like some other teachers do. Kate let us put our ideas into the ideas' (Anton). 'I might take a bit of someone's ideas and put it in my story; it's making more ideas and it's a bit different and juggling around with ideas' (Amandeep) (Yr5-T).

Where pupils see themselves as active learners, permitted to tackle increasingly more difficult tasks and developing their skills year by year, learning has become a process internalised within their life histories. Work where pupils have not felt in control of the learning, by definition, has little meaning and it fails to engage them.

> I think of their idea and how I could change it but then suddenly the idea gives me a completely different idea in my head and then I use that idea and see if it works. I get the ideas from walking home or things at home such as playing games, computer games and things like that. I just get moves from them and make up my ideas from those moves.
>
> (Corin, Yr5-V)

Environments of high risk and high ambiguity are needed (Pollard 1990) to ensure young participants control and the provision of opportunities for fantasy and imagination to work. Uncertainty coupled with fear is less likely to encourage risk taking. The Reggio schools (Emilia 1996) maintain that children enjoy balances and imbalances, they yearn to discover measures and relations of complex situations, ever seeking the art of pleasures, transgressing measures and relations, changing their meanings, creating their own analogies and metaphors and yet seeking realistic answers and logical meanings. They are on a voyage of discovery:

> Kate, the drama teacher from the National Theatre exploring historical literature as part of their Tudor history project, introduces some everyday items to the Yr5 class, such as a brush, a cloth and a ball. She asks the children to give her ideas about how these might be used for making puppets and for the sounds that the puppets might make. Hamish says the brush looks like a forest. Toby says that the cloth was similar to the one that goes on a hot water cylinder. She moves the brush around and the children listen to the sounds it makes: 'It sounds like a snake, like a lavatory cleaner, like a cockroach.' They suggest they could use the non-bouncing ball as Sloth, one of the characters in the Faust play. They are then asked to apply one of the objects to a character. Zizzi says the ball could be a lazy, fat, big headed, bored person and that the nail brush could be a hairy chested dancer.
>
> (FN-4/03/04-Yr5-T)

Learners become immersed in this phase of adventures in their historical drama: 'You can actually do your imagination' (Cody, Yr5-T). The taking over of a character is an open imaginative adventure that brings a significant element of control to the learner: 'You could use your imagination to create the person yourself, like what they look like' (Sophie). 'You help it become more creative, to make it much more fun for people' (Cody) (Yr5-T).

Creative teachers encourage imaginative adventures: 'My passion is about putting young people in a position where they can find a way of expressing something they might not have known they wanted to express and didn't know was possible. I don't say "this is a painting project or a flag making project" but we start in a physical way. We were making mini beasts in science in Yr1 and they were making themselves into dragonflies so they could understand the different bits of a dragonfly' (Teacher artist Sam-T).

Learners have personal connections or individual ideas that heighten their motivation: 'I like being creative. I like making different pictures, drawings and sketches because I have got a good imagination. When I draw I come out with queer ideas like space ships and when writing a story I think about the future and then I have a story. My mum has told me that I'm imaginative. I'll make anything that nobody else has made' (Henry, Yr6-S).

Their imagination is allowed to take over as in this description of their design and technology project of a playground structure:

When you go in here you could either sit down here or you could go in the museum that leads to the infant playground. If you're working on Victorians or something there's all different things you can learn about in your lesson. There are seats inside as well that are museum kind of seats and interesting things that you sit on like shoes. It's just like a photo gallery, there are different titles, a picture of each one for each year and a bit of information and we're going to have a projector showing different pictures, pictures that we make because they're going to be our ideas.

(Abdul, Yr5-T)

They quickly brought their own experiences, references and resources to a situation (Jeffrey 2002): 'If I read a book like Harry Potter it will give me an idea such as to eat slugs. I get ideas from the music; if it's relaxing I might do some relaxing movements' (Tash). 'I did it from things at home, I'm walking home playing games, computer games and things like that, and I get moves from them and make up my ideas for those moves' (Corin). They were not averse to using others' ideas: 'I think of their idea and how I could change it but then suddenly the idea gives me a completely different idea in my head and then I use that idea and see if it works' (Lottie) (Yr6-V).

They get carried along with the adventure even if their control is occasionally more spontaneous than structured: 'When I play a character I feel really excited but I think that I'm not going to be able to say the word. It's creative and if you were a character like Pluto you enjoy yourself and if you forget the lines and you don't have the script you just make it up as you go along through the story' (Duran, Yr5-T).

Learners are keen to develop complexity in imaginative investigations. Yr5 learners were given the task of developing star shapes by drawing lines between six equidistant points on a circle during the Maths Trail: 'It's fun seeing how far you can get, putting in more lines and making it more complex'; 'The colouring is less important than making a complex pattern' (Yr5-S).

The development of a complexity through the imagination may well emerge for bounded tasks:

> The Robin Hood Game as part of a design and technology project involving problem solving, literacy and numeracy: 'The aim is to finish the trail successfully with as many lives left as possible. The game has three parts. There is the race to finish, trying to stay alive in the game and collecting as many lives as possible. The game is a complex one which has a race, an "in and out" part and a lives count. I got carried away when I started. I liked doing it because I had the independence to do what I wanted and I could make up the rules' (Ruby).
>
> (Yr6-S)

Solving a problem within a creative and imaginative context requires a great deal of attention to detail for the process is constrained and bounded by the original frame as in the construction of a maths game for younger children by a group in Yr6:

> 'And we're going to have a metal structure to hold it up this time and it's going to be 2m wide 'cos it's an equal square so the sides are going to be 2m and the height is going to be 1.5m high so it's not too hard for little children to reach' (Didier). 'There's going to be like a board for the umpire and the umpire might call up a sum and you've got to find the jigsaw piece with the answer on it and that might be the first piece to go in the side or the other side or just in the middle. For instance, 11 times 2 for Yr6, 2 times 20 for Yr5, 8 times 2 for Yr 4 and 1 times 2 for Yr1' (Jordan). 'They'll pick up on their times tables and sums and they'll get faster if they go on longer' (Didier). 'They'll also make friends, 'cos they have to work together and if they have partners on the pyramid they can work together more and more' (Jordan).
>
> (Yr6-T)

Problem solving, like excitement and pleasure, can only be considered a major feature of creative learning if there is an element of control and innovation in the process. Yr5 were asked to estimate how many grains of sand there were on a picture as part of a maths investigation into estimating and to provide details of the methods used to solve the problem: 'I counted the grains of sand in a small area and then multiplied the number of small areas'; 'I did columns and rows'; 'I put a line across and down and multiplied'; 'I circled and counted the number in each circle'; 'I think I had about a 100 cubes of sand' (Yr6-S).

Across imaginative adventures, investigations and solution seeking these learners have employed a range of creative learning features – manipulation, comparison, experimentation, framework development, instantaneous ideas, risk taking, co-participation, complexity development, simplicity extraction, recursiveness and patterning.

Moulding and crafting: the developmental phase

During this stage outcomes are produced based on structured support, a developed knowledge of the situation and activity and its possibilities. However, there are also frustrations with which to grapple and accommodations and compromises to make. These are the final constructions of something worthwhile, purposeful and imaginative – one definition of creative learning (NACCCE 1999). Time is an essential element of this phase:

> It's partly the way both myself and Frank [sculptor] work. The work is quite organic. We haven't gone into any class and said this is what we're going to do. We've gone and said 'what shall we do? What's possible?' The most successful ones have been the ones where we have had most time, there's a real story behind the final product, the design process, the investigation of ideas and themes and trips out to see other places and it added into this sense that we are all on a journey.
>
> (Teacher artist Sam-T)

The most extensive crafting project of the research was the construction of playground shelters in a design and technology project involving maths, problem solving and collaboration:

> The group who are designing the playground seats use a tablet PC and the Paint software. I asked the children what they could do on a tablet. 'You select your preferred activity such as writing with a specific font or you rub-out or draw. The pen does this selection.' When they go into the playground they discuss with a teacher where they should put their seats. They decided they should go around the curved fence made with two foot high logs. They decide not to put them by the bins because it would smell. They then took digital photographs of the places where they were going to put their seats. Each pair of children were photographed in that place. The photographs were transferred to the tablets and the children designed the seats on and around these photographs.
>
> (FN-26/02/04-T)

Young participants moulded their products just as sculptors, potters, stone masons and weavers shape and fashion their works of art, as in this wildlife science project involving media presentations:

> These are big cats in the bush. I liked the drawing and making up big facts and it's my favourite topic – animals and birds. I've liked animals all my life. I read loads of books full of information. I think it is creative. The yellow and brown stripes right across the page is quite creative. It puts me in mind of the big cats who have those kinds of stripes.
>
> (Hamish, Yr5-T)

The learners give life to their expressions, e.g. through the moulding of movement in the beginning of the universe science project through dance:

> 'We had to do a roll and a jump and the jump was the shooting star and one was the meteorite and it was like you hit into it, like you were really angry' (Gemma). 'The shooting star was like a run and jump. It was just like shooting off, into a different place and then settling again and the next time it was going to shoot off you ran and jumped' (Ashaquell). 'Venus was all peaceful like a garden and Mars was like a war ground with guns around like Iraq and America. Terminating' (Issaka).
>
> (Yr5-V)

And they give life to a curriculum demand to construct a 3D useful object in design and technology incorporating manipulative skills and cooperation:

> 'I am putting an antenna on my hat so it looks funny because it's a funny hat. I like jokes. I'm going to make eyes and a mouth and I'm going to use bubble wrap as stiffener and pipe cleaners for the antenna with a bobble on the top' (Callum). One boy asks another one how he made a semicircle and he gets a pencil and some string and shows him how to draw an ark. 'I want my hat to be a Manchester United hat. I am going to fold it over, put on some red ribbon and a bell on the string connected to my hand' (Jordan).
>
> (FN-4/02/04-Yr6-T)

Moulding involved deftness, adroitness and nimbleness in any active project such as the dance-universe exercise:

> 'You're in a group and you have to stay together and one is Earth and one is Mars and there are people lying on the floor and people had to run around like they were rotating. Venus and Mars were rotating round the sun' (Gemma). 'We had partners and they dropped to the floor and we had to dodge everyone and jump over them. Like rotating,

spinning around or going round it. And you had to open and close and keep on doing it, and if you were going forward and there was someone in the way you had to try and open and then close and try to go to the right or left' (Kalvin).

(Yr5-V)

They gradually graft their experiences and others' ideas into their own expressions, sequences, compositions and narratives: 'I use other people's ideas and I change it a bit' (Corin, Yr5-H).

Work was not something to be avoided but to embrace even if it was arduous, strenuous and exacting:

'You have to keep on practising the same thing and you start to think "do you have to keep on?" when you have to keep your arms up for a long time in a difficult shape. It starts to get hard keeping that shape' (Lottie). 'You have to keep your arms in the air and you're dying to get them down and you're aching and feel you can't do any more' (Corin). 'It's all the same basically, you start to strain when you are bending down and he says try and hold it for a bit longer' (Carl). 'What happens with me is after two times of stretching and opening and closing my legs ache and the teacher keeps pushing us until our legs feel all floppy' (Nichel). 'It was sometimes uncomfortable and painful. You get really stuffy inside you, your face starts to get really hot, your heart starts to beat faster and if you have to do a pose for a long time your muscles start to ache' (Marianne).

(Yr6-H)

They were not averse to arduous activity: 'I don't mind being pushed. Sometimes you have to put a lot of effort into things that you haven't done before and I think it's really good actually' (Will). They were 'trying to show that we are capable of trying to do something hard, testing our balancing skills. We wanted to do our best' (Marianne). Their determination and resoluteness was rewarded by the progress made: 'It is tiring after the first few seconds, then you keep doing it and keep getting used to it and suddenly it starts to get easier so I like doing shapes, it's a very good way of relaxing as well as it makes you tired' (Corin) (Yrs5+6-H).

Their experience of authentic labour was all-consuming:

When you're properly into the thing you're making or doing, you're concentrating and you're liking what you're building, you just keep on, you can't get out of it, you're just stuck with the thing you're doing, thinking what you're doing and you're enjoying it because you are making more. If you weren't concentrating you would just go 'I don't want to do this any more, I can't be bothered'.

(Anton, Yr5-T)

The whole experience was one of contrastive engagements, of rigorous and relentless striving contrasted with periods of relaxation and reflection. The search for peak experience produced integrity of process.

> The children are learning how to work in a circle, going in and out and circling round in different directions. Their faces are serious as they have to concentrate on the beat and the direction of turn when the circle goes round in the opposite direction. They are learning about unity and unison in the universe. As they practise their universe 'birth and sound' sequence they watch the leader with a studied intent as they perform the flash jump, the smooth roll, the scrunch role and the flame leap. Their eyes follow their arms looking into space with slow stretched turns. Nadine smiles as she explodes and follows this with a spiky roll and a swirl.
>
> (FN-21/11/03-V)

Their peak experience has been a product of their exertion, determination and inspiration to fulfil the joy of performance and in doing so they had reached a pinnacle of collective endeavour: 'The dance teacher claps them all at the end of the session and they all break out into clapping themselves with heightened excitement' (FN-9/03/04-H).

Conclusion

Scaffolding by teachers, which included loosening constraints, devising a range of hands-on activities and providing the appropriate atmosphere and resources, led to participants taking over learning processes as they familiarised themselves with the situation, used their imagination in a mediating phase, and finally moulded and crafted the end product. In this way there is a gradual increase in control of the learning process by the participants through which they eventually take ownership of the fruits of their learning. This is the subject of the next chapter.

3 Ownership of knowledge

Ownership of knowledge results when young participants learn for them-selves, not just for the teacher, examiner or society. Knowledge becomes meaningful to them within their own personal frame of reference, not one dictated by external assessment. Learning activity is also internalised as being owned by them (Woods *et al.* 1999). Knowledge becomes an integral part of the pupil's self and identity, and it is through these that we consider the issue of ownership in this chapter.

Ownership is the internalisation of learning experience, the develop-ment of the competent individual who gains public recognition and enjoys telling others (Woods *et al.* 1999), gaining a real sense of achievement and developing feelings of personal worth (Breakwell 1986). There is thus both an internal and an external aspect. Pollard and Filer (1999) show this in their analysis of learner identity consisting of three contributing groups of factors – potential, resources, and relationship of self to others. Potential is the biological endowment, resources are the role of material, cultural and linguistic factors – exemplified in the last chapter on control – and relationship of self and others is the subject of this chapter.

The social context for creative learning in our research was the basis for the development of an ownership that was meaningful, just as scaffolding framed the development of control over learning. We consider these social contexts in the first part of the chapter, before going on to consider the learner's developing identity – and the gathering sense of ownership – in the second part.

Social learning

The development of participative cultures for creative learning built upon the social nature of the young participants. The creative learning strategies adopted by the teachers in the partner projects mainly focused on shared engagements. The longitudinal PACE project in the 1990s showed that where these social relations were reduced, learning became less meaningful and the value for learning became more instrumental, as did the social rela-tions. Personal interactions are valued more than teaching and learning qualifications (Pollard *et al.* 2000), and learners are happiest when interests and identity are accommodated (Pollard and Filer 1999). The emotional benefit of positive social relations was a major contributor to the development of ownership of knowledge.

As well as contributing to the participative culture, the learners' role was to take risks and experiment, to have a go and to craft their products to perfection over long periods of time, to be resourceful and to share ideas. This increased decision making for learners, between learners and between teachers and learners. They became appreciators of creativity itself and of each other's ideas, commitments and products. They were allowed to colonise physical space, virtual space through the Internet and intellectual space and then to release the spaces for others or others' ideas. Their social role was to add value to the creative learning situation for each other and for the development of knowledge and learning and the success of this was evidenced in their enthusiasm for returning to the creative learning situations set up by both their teachers and themselves.

Our research identified three types of social participation – co-participative, collaborative and collective – which we shall consider in turn. The first is a social situation in which individuals are acting creatively by themselves but drawing upon the social context for ideas to include or reject and at the same time developing a feeling of belonging to the whole group and social context. In the second, the collaborative, a group work together in a creative activity and sometimes act co-participatively using the social context as a resource. Collective participation involves the whole class acting together to construct something or learners contributing to a class situation involving the attention and engagement of the whole class.

Co-participation

Co-participation has been used to describe the interactive relationship between teachers and learners in which they both investigate and develop the process of teaching and learning together (Emilia 1996). It also fits a process, found in our research, where learners investigate a learning experience that is embedded in a social learning context of the classroom. The young learners worked as co-participators – working individually or in groups but drawing on the whole creative environment where individuals or groups cast around the room or space for ideas without formal collaborations. At the same time they acted as a resource for other individuals and groups, 'If you can't think of anything really good you look at someone else and you just think of something and it just comes into your head' (Isabelle, Yr5-V). This practice created an appreciative ethos (Jeffrey 2001a): 'You could almost feel everyone in the class acknowledge that that was an interesting, unusual thing' (Dance teacher-H).

Learners can act individually but draw upon the community of learners of a classroom just as adults use books, media, histories and other people to act creatively, as in the following case of Yr4 learners engaged in a design and technology and science investigation. They were making a can holder with malleable foam that retains its shape when heated as part of a science lesson investigating whether plasticine is waterproof or not through testing:

> We cut out four templates and then mould them and stick them together with the glue guns and then we heat them up and then remodelled them and they stay like our design. I made my bottom different to everyone else's. I didn't want it to be the same as others. It's boring doing what others do. I wanted to see what things look like when it's not the same as the others. I do a little bit of what others do and then I do my own idea. I copied Alexander's zigzag but made my base slope upwards. There's nothing wrong with copying what everyone else does but I like to add my own ideas. I like to add my own ideas.
>
> (Martin, Yr4-S)

Here, learners are using the resources generated by others to develop and critique their own constructions and problems. The comparison with others clearly demonstrates that what emerges is theirs and theirs alone.

While carrying out individual tasks in a co-participative context, learners often take the opportunity to use social relations to investigate the task in more depth, using their experiences as subjects for conversation, just as adults might:

> Andrea the teacher refers to an artist they have looked at in the past and she gives them each a large flower which they have to draw. As the children look at it they discuss what they know about flowers. 'That's the pollen. I remember when it fell over me, it stains the clothes.' 'If you put it on yourself bees will come after you for that is what they want.' 'It makes a scent, which is what they really want.' 'My mum's friend owns a gallery and we threw flowers in a pond. I have seen giant daisies in my neighbour's garden.' 'Creativity stands for art and cooking.' 'Flowers, trees and bushes can be used by people to be creative.' 'Creativity is creating more things, poems and stories.' Nadia says to Emmanuel: 'Why don't you rub the pastel with your finger? I prefer that look because the shade of the colour comes out.' He says thank you gratefully: 'Creativity is my hobby.'
>
> (FN-12/11/03-Yr4-T)

Creative learning can be enhanced by the sociability of the context. Learners tend to notice interesting and unusual things when they see them in someone else. 'I don't know if you remember those two boys who did a balance on their knees. You could almost feel everyone in the class acknowledge that that was an interesting, unusual thing that they'd not seen before' (Dance teacher-H). Here we see a kind of collective ownership whereby pupils as a class have generated knowledge of some kind, and which they can all internalise, as well as specific ones to the boys in question. We see more of this in what follows.

Collaborative participation

Collaborative projects were where learners actually worked together in small groups or pairs to produce something or solve a problem. 'You could have rubbish small ideas and you put them together to make a big one' (Andrea, Yr5-V). Ideas and possibilities were matured or declared obsolete: 'When you're working together you can throw that idea away, get rid of it, or if the other one's got an idea and you've got an idea, they can go together or you can use them in different parts of the sequence' (Toni, Yr6-V).

Participants drew upon the storm of ideas and interactions and gained support from it, as well as imbibing a culture of appreciation and creativity as they operate a workshop approach (Woods and Jeffrey 1996):

> They are researching the Tudors following their work on Dr. Faustus. Some are using the Google search engine to look up Tudor ships and others are designing ships on their tablets. One group work very closely as a social unit. 'We should applaud Duran for finding the English Victory ship on the Internet,' says Mickey. Joe finds something relevant to Greenwich and Mickey says 'nice find'. Mickey says, 'I'm going to give you a new job, Joe. Find a web site with loads of text and select what we want and then download it to Microsoft Word and Duran will print it.' Nathan draws, Duran and Joe use the tablets to seek facts, and Mickey supervises, co-ordinates, organises, facilitates and stimulates: 'I'm still looking for more, is that okay Mickey?' says Joe.
> (FN-1/03/04-Yr5-T)

Collective ownership emerges as they all contribute. Pairs or groups worked collaboratively to make up a sequence or narrative but they also worked co-participatively casting around the room to make use of other expressions they felt appropriate for the construction of their group sequences. They also contributed to evaluations of others' compositions and to the development of class themes. Their interactive collaborations made the role of evaluator part of the joy of creative learning:

> 'It's fun and it's good to be co-operative and you can talk to each other and you can make things, share ideas, put them together and then something good might happen so it's good to share ideas' (Ikran). 'I don't think it's true that working on your own will produce better ideas. If you have good ideas maybe the other person will have good ideas and together you'll make them better' (Tashi).
> (Yr5-V)

They got emotional and intellectual support and evaluation from each other as they formulated innovative sequences: 'I think team work is really good; if you didn't work with each other you wouldn't have anyone to support you and tell you that you're doing well and also tell you that you have better ideas. I'm not sure about anybody else but it makes me think better when I'm working with a group. I work better with a group' (Will). The support assisted the development of a culture focused on celebrating innovation: 'They might learn something from the other person if they're not so good. If you share ideas you are being helpful and you are making them feel proud of themselves. You're making them happy and you are also proud of what you have taught them' (Maryanne) (Yr5-V).

In their collaborations leaders emerged, as in this design and technology project involving computer studies, maths and art in a Tudor project:

> They then took digital photographs of the places where they were going to put their seat designs in the playground. Each pair of children was photographed in that place. The photographs were transferred to the computer tablets and the children designed the seats on and around these photographs. Sophie asked Rodney, 'What would you like behind the seat? What colours would you like?' He said he would like 'big bushes behind the seats'. Sophie said, 'I don't mind going last and putting your ideas in first.' She continues to construct the design while asking Rodney and Bethany what they want. She asks Rodney if he would like apple trees, how big he would like them to be and whether they wanted it to cover the whole space. She apologises because it is so messy. She asks Bethany whether she would like an acorn tree or an apple tree. She suggests that as Rodney wants squirrels in the picture it is an acorn tree as squirrels eat acorns like piglet in Winnie the Pooh.
>
> (FN-23/03/04-T)

Self-esteem is promoted on both sides here. The collaborating dynamics between the participants consisted of interactions where ideas and possibilities were matured or cast away as obsolete: 'When you're working together you can throw that idea away, get rid of it, or if the other one's got an idea and you've got an idea they can go together or you can use them in different parts of the sequence. So if they think walking is not right you can spin around to give it more action. Then you could use the walking. They could spin around in the centre and you could walk round them so you're doing different parts of the earth and sun' (Lottie, Yr6-V).

Their interactive dynamism was linguistic, corporeal, emotional and physical, not just intellectual:

> They practised being innovative in groups and negotiated as they acted or stood still and looked at each other for inspiration or looked around or followed the other, chatting with their hands as they demonstrated:

During the whole class demonstration they watch intently. They discuss, think, argue, volunteer, pull, push, show, experiment, point,
follow, instruct, explain, cajole, stare, look quizzical, hand demonstrate, clap, mouth, count, explode with excitement, laugh, shift from
seriousness to delight and then focus intently with eyeball engagements.
(FN-9/03/04-Yr6-H)

Ownership involves having choice within a democratic framework. Their
collaborations involved 'negotiation, working with two people, and some of
that negotiation will be about making choices' (Dance teacher-H). In collaborative groups they constantly negotiated constructions without rancour:
'You want to go at the top of the first pile and at other times you want to go
here and there. You just work it out between you. We just talk and don't
shout to get our way' (Mazie, Yr5-V). Collaborations are not always successful as some of the dance participants recognised: 'When I was in my
group I wanted to make it perfect but they kept on talking about other stuff,
we only had about 10 or 20 minutes and the teacher was counting quite fast,
and I wanted to get it perfect' (Katie, Yr6-V). Collaborations, like collective
participations, have a value added element as their relationships develop and
in a reciprocal manner the quality of their learning is enhanced:

They're learning to co-operate. It makes it funny when they put their
ideas together, like once when Nina and I were together and we were trying to do a forward slash and Kevin was doing a cartwheel and David
couldn't do a hand stand and kept on messing up the dance and it made
it funnier. It's good because at the end you feel happy about the dance and
you feel like you want to show it to people and you're happy about them.
(Maryanne, Yr5-V)

Participants are active in the construction and negotiation of lives, pursuing
both social and learning goals (Pollard and Filer 1999). They debated and
argued:

How you do it is that you work with someone you know you're going
to be good with, who has ideas similar to you but if they disagree with
you, you have to start talking to each other. Most of the time people do
agree with you. Sometimes, if they don't agree you have to put different
ideas together and then you make a sequence. It feels good because then
you know you've done something well and you haven't just told them
to do what you wanted to do. You used their ideas as well.
(Lottie, Yr6-V)

The interactions were often more dynamic when different contexts were
experienced: 'Usually we work with the same people and we know what
they're going to do but when you're with different people you can see the
different way they do things' (Maryanne, Yr5-V).

The process of creating an expression, sequence or narrative collectively or collaboratively was seen as providing more opportunities to innovate because self-reflective debates are less appropriate for young participants (Wegerif 2002):

> I think that, at this stage, working with a partner or in a trio is actually much more effective because it allows them to debate their work as they're going along with another person. I think having that debate with themselves is a more sophisticated thing to deal with, which maybe they're not ready for it yet. It allows them to have a debate about choices with another real live person.
>
> (Dance teacher-V)

Collective participations

They went on to work as collective participants as a whole class, designing and fashioning projects:

> They can all see each other. It has that democratic element to it – and I can also see them. So you can very quickly ascertain who is not concentrating and who is. It just seems to focus everyone's energy in that way, so that when they then turn to face me, they're ready to go through a series of things that they feel vaguely familiar with. Somehow it seems to set the tone quite well. And also doing their own movement seems to set the mood in terms of being creative. You know you will be expected to come up with something different and new, and try something out. I try and acknowledge those people that are trying something they may not have tried before.
>
> (Dance teacher-H)

All the sessions had parts where groups carried out demonstrations to the rest of the class who acted as an audience, but an informed one:

> The teacher asks the class for a comment after each presentation. The children noted the different levels, movements on the floor, jumps in unexpected places, unexpected jumps at the beginning from air to floor: 'I liked the bit where their feet met the floor, when they jumped across each other.' One group stopped in the middle and began to argue as they went back to their places but nobody said anything.
>
> (FN-5/02/04-H)

These collective interactions developed an appreciation of each other's worth. The sense of ownership is strengthened if it is acknowledged by others:

When they're watching others work they'll watch each other and maybe smile or laugh or say something or go 'ooh that's good'. I think it's about acknowledging in each other that they've done something that is interesting or humorous, or something that provokes a positive response. You can see that in the audience and then you can see that reflected in the performer, that they have created this thing that has provoked that response.

(Dance teacher-H)

Knowledge that is owned is not bland and unquestioned. Collective practices stimulate not only supportive, but also critical, assessments and evaluations as in this discussion of proposals to make the playground seating:

Once again the whole class gathers together to discuss each other's design, asking questions and commenting. The learners tell the others what materials would be used to construct their design, e.g.: fibre glass and red gel, colour film, plastic, steel spikes, steel boxes for the game numbers, sprayed or painted glass, sponge, Velcro.

(FN-9/03/04-Yr6-T)

In particular pedagogic cultures, collective enquiry and critique is essential (Woods and Jeffrey 1996). It extends and connects knowledge:

In the maths session, Anton spots that Graham has repeated a sum on the white board. They are finding rules to apply to a computation. For example, 11 times 4 equals 44 so doubling either multiplier doubles the result. Graham asks the children 'what has been my job?' Mickey says, 'to show how things we know are connected'.

(FN-21/01/04-Yr5-T)

Engagements with teachers were sometimes more co-participative in that each individual or group were working on their own but classroom collectivity was engaged at appropriate moments:

Learners could be heard quietly anticipating the teacher's next move or instruction and if highlighted these could be drawn into the co-participative engagement. She discussed with the learners the reasons for using this particular tool, inviting them to take ownership of the activity.

(FN-17/03/03-Yr6-S)

Using the experience, perspectives and imagination of young participants teachers are able to construct a collective participatory culture:

The teacher then asked them what they knew about 'pop art'. She accepted all contributions offered and recorded them on her white board. Her pedagogic style was not 'elicitation' – displaying what she wished to be recorded by choosing the appropriate comments from the children. She accepted all the contributions but she emphasised the one she thought was correct and relevant. Some of the children have developed a style of asking if a possibility might be correct, perhaps to prevent themselves from being castigated for being wrong.

(FN-17/03/04-Yr6-S)

Learners' contributions were clearly accepted as valid and rejection of their contributions was not considered part of the teacher's pedagogy. In this way what is often called class teaching becomes a collective participative experience of creative learning. It is against this social backdrop that learners take ownership of their learning through the development of their learning identity.

Developing ownership and identity

The development of a social identity was crucial to the development of a positive relationship between self and learning. The incorporation of the learners' life experiences into the development and understanding of curriculum programmes was felt to be important to the young participants. Pollard and Filer (1999) described young children's learning career as 'a continuous spiral' in which identity is seen as a representation of the self-belief and self-confidence which learners bring to new learning challenges and contexts. However, they also identified an aspect of self and identity that is concerned with 'what they *become* through interaction with significant others, their experience of new learning opportunities and their engagement with dominant social representations within their culture' (Pollard and Filer 1999, p. 22, original emphasis).

Creative learning contributed to the construction and development of learners' social identities but learners interpreted and shaped their personal identity (Pollard and Filer 1999). Young participants in our research engaged meaningfully with learning when they had an opportunity to control the processes with which they were engaged and own the knowledge they encountered. These situations provided assurances that manifestations of their 'selves' as individual and unique learners were valued and safe in that personal perspectives, and what might at times be seen as idiosyncrasies, were acceptable and contributed to the general dynamic culture. In this way they felt free to be creative. They felt able to act independently, although at the same time they appreciated teachers' advice and support. In this process they played with their identities, gradually moulding them and remoulding them according to the learning situation and to the social context.

Their learning identity development had three main aspects to it: playing with identities, achievement and a sense of place. Each in turn fostered a developing sense of ownership.

Playing with identities

Pollard and Filer (1999) use a typology to describe the way primary children engage with and negotiate the structures and expectations embedded in schooling – conformity, anti-conformity, non-conformity and redefining. The last is the one that is most apparent in creative learning situations:

> *Redefining* is associated with the same mainstream patterns of achievement and cultural norms as *conformity*. However, pupils using *redefining* strategies are not so much operating *within* norms and expectations as at the cutting edge of them. They are pushing at the boundaries of teachers' and peers' expectation, negotiating, challenging and leading their peers. This is a strategy which is only viable for pupils where their structural position in a class is high with regard to their academic and social status.
>
> (ibid., p. 27, italics in original)

This suggests that redefining is only available to the best pupils. We found, however, that creative learning contexts allow the possibility of *redefinition* for all young participants to some degree, giving all the chance to push the boundaries and challenge and lead their peers. Challenges are examples of self-determination and self-reinforcement (Woods 1995) and agency in operation: 'I prefer the challenge and failing. I've failed a few times and now it is easier' (Patrick, Yr5-S). Young participants cannot compare earlier types of curriculum provision easily for they do not have the resources to do this but they can comment on bits and pieces they experience and they can talk about forms they find challenging or limiting (Rudduck *et al.* 2004). Playing with identity provided young participants with an opportunity to play with the relationship between self and social identity: 'I am less shy in life from my experience of drama. If I think something is wrong like I don't want to play a game, I go into a character and don't walk off' (Frankie, Yr5-T).

The Faustus history project over ten weeks culminating in a performance at a local theatre added to the opportunity for play:

> 'It made me happy after it because it filled up a space in my body and they cheered and that felt nice. You get to understand more about each other. We worked together and sometimes we talked together and you understand each other better.' The situation allowed an opportunity for

reflection and redefinition of their spiral identity career: 'I liked it because I can be another person because I don't really like my own character, my own self.'

(Mickey, Yr5-T)

Play involved reflecting upon these games: 'I wanted to do things because it's exciting but then afterwards I realised that I didn't like it so I regretted it. Sometimes I don't want to show off and some activities make me seem like I am doing so' (Frankie, Yr5-T). They were developing moral and ethical criteria for the establishment of their identities through the curriculum: 'You reap what you sow. The more effort you put in to something like the Tudor portraits the more pleasure and proudness you get out' (Amandeep, Yr5-T). Their engagement with the Faustus and Tudor history projects brought them face to face with moral dilemmas that became meaningful for them: 'He [Faustus] gave up his soul so he could do anything he wanted for twenty-four years and there were just a few minutes when the good angel came and said he could still change his mind and the bad angel said, "No, you've made a deal, you can't"' (Usha, Yr5-T). They discussed what they would have done:

'I think it would be really tempting to have done anything you wanted. You could fly or whatever, to do stuff that no human could do, but I still wouldn't have done that' (Reece). 'I would have listened to the good angel and remembered how I used to be and then handed it back after the first month' (Usha). 'I would have turned it down because it's not worth it because everything you'd always done wouldn't be there any more and you'd feel more pain. He would be in Hell and that would be pain. Hell is really bad. They poke you with little hot sticks and make you eat cockroaches' (Hamish).

(Yr5-T)

These experiences and analysis carried over into their writing: 'I think that at this age the more emotionally mature children do start to reflect upon description and detail of people's emotions in their writing' (Graham, Deputy Head-T). They identified with characters: 'I would have preferred to play Ferdinand than Prospero because there was more emotion in him. When acting it's better to have emotions than just to be cruel and bossy' (Zizzi, Yr5-T).

Teachers who use learner inclusiveness accept the limits of their perspectives and embrace those of students (MacBeath *et al.* 2003), combining the social process of identity development and learning. Identities were played with in order to develop empathy and understanding and to develop the art of defence as exemplified by role playing during the Tudor topic:

When the video has installed Graham asks for someone to take the role of a Catholic. As the volunteer walks to the front of the class some children call him 'traitor'. The children have to think up some questions to ask him:

'Would you fight in the war?' 'No.'
'Why are you in our country?' 'Because I live here but I do not want to betray the Catholic countries.'
'If Spain invades would you say you are on their side?' 'Yes.'
'Would you feel OK if Spain won?' 'Yes.'
'How do you earn money now you are confined to your home?' 'Inside the house.'
'Supposing the opposition paid you, would you give up your faith?' 'No.'

(FN-3/02/04-Yr5-T)

Playing with identities aids confidence as learners try out social interactions and engagements and bring their positive experiences to other demanding situations as exemplified by reactions to the dance project aimed at increasing confidence:

It's fun and when you're actually sharing it with other people it builds up your confidence, it brings you out. I built more confidence in myself and I can now show what I'm capable of and I've become more confident in what I'm doing. It's helped me in class because a lot of the time I never used to put my hand up because I was afraid that I would get it wrong and now this project has brought my confidence up.

(Nicholas, Yr6-H)

As the identity develops, becomes more secure and blossoms in new directions, ownership of knowledge deepens and becomes more extensive.

Achievement

Learners liked to achieve for themselves and creative learning gave them the opportunity to internalise the ownership of their labour and give them the confidence of being a competent individual. The social context of creative learning added public recognition (Woods *et al.* 1999):

When I finish a piece of work, I feel I've achieved something. Like, when I'd finished my map, I felt, like, it's a whole block of work. I just thought, 'Wow! That's really good!' If you look at it up on the wall you sort of say 'That's mine'. If you did it quite a long time ago, you can, if there's something on your table that you're just finishing and it's something slightly like that on the wall, you can look at it and you can compare them to see if you've progressed.

(Madeline, Yr5-SL)

Achievement was therefore central to becoming a worthy learner: 'I won't work hard if it isn't fun but my main rule is I like hard work if it pays off in the end' (Amandeep, Yr5-T). The design and construction of a covered playground seat, which was actually built with the help of the young participants by the project art facilitator from the girls' designs, enhanced their learning identities: 'I like working hard because at the end you or someone else is going to be proud of me. I think it's a nice feeling to have someone say "that's really nice, you tackled that really well, you found that hard but you still did it"' (Freya, Yr5-T).

Where the close relationship between self and achievement is mirrored well-being is engendered:

I am going to make a complicated design so I can see the shapes. I started putting on shapes going round and then attaching them to the middle of the plate with the sellotape. Then I decided to do a spider's web with string and then I added more bits. I felt happy because I kept on doing it and doing it until I stopped.

(Natasha, Yr6-S)

Creative learning appears to be effective learning and for young participants it is therefore worthwhile making an investment: 'My sister just went through GCSE and she had history and apparently she remembered what she had done in primary school. You get something out of it at the end' (Zizzi, Yr5-T). 'It showed me if you work hard at something you get something out of it; at the end you achieve something' (Amandeep, Yr5-T).

Connections with personal experiences of family life made school learning more relevant which in turn promoted ownership (see also Chapter 1):

I am doing cross stitch at home. I am making some kneelers for the church in cross stitch. I have been doing it for a few years. I liked doing design and technology in Yr4 when we made some purses. I had a difficult design with one on one side and another design on the other side. It was therefore twice the amount of sewing but I thought it was interesting. It made it challenging. It was good because I had to think about it and work out how to do it.

(Louie, Yr6-T)

Intellectual rigour also made learning meaningful and developed the learners' identities at the same time:

It's a challenge. You have to keep at it. It's something you have to finish in the time available. You have to think about it and concentrate on it. When you finish it you have learnt something and achieved your goal and when you come back to it again you know what it means.

(Jordan, Yr6-S)

Achievement also represents that distinctiveness and uniqueness (Breakwell 1986), that self-determination (Woods 1995) and the need and desire to avoid being indistinct (Emilia 1996): 'I am proud of not being like everyone else. This D+T construction belongs to me. I own it' (Joseph, Yr6-S).

A sense of place

Learners need time and space to develop a secure and positive learning identity (Breakwell 1986). Creative learning projects and similar approaches to classroom organisation and culture, particularly in the primary school with its year-long class system, contribute positively to this experience. The opportunity to be a redefiner rather than a conformist, non-conformist or anti-conformist (Pollard and Filer 1999) depends on the sense of ownership learners have over the space within which they are placed by the institution.

Learners' sense of place was specifically influential in the way many of the activities made use of the school environment, such as the dance floor, the drama space, corridors for exhibitions, specialist art rooms, the school grounds, the presentations and the 'real' projects:

I am with Frank, the sculptor, and some Year 1 children. They are painting poles like telegraph poles for the construction of a butterfly and insect house. This is their contribution to the Grounded in Colour project with science base – mini beasts. First of all they roll them along a track and stamp and clap and count to eight to set the roll going. It is a vigorous activity 'to gather all this energy' (Frank, Artist-T). As they paint the poles they contribute ideas, 'why don't we make a door at that end?', and analysis: 'it looks interesting', 'it looks like a boat', 'it looks like an airplane', 'it looks like a ski run', 'it looks like a bridge'.

(FN-10/03/04-T)

Encouraging learners to engage in creative learning in different physical contexts promoted a sense of ownership of each new place:

The cooking we did yesterday in the school kitchen was hands on and they were seeing results straight away and you keep their attention and they really do focus on what they're doing. An awful lot of learning going on, that's how we present Foundation curriculum, mainly through hands-on activity. The same happened in numeracy week. We went out to the community and looked at patterns around, out and about. Children were bursting with creativity because they were bringing things like patchwork patterns on cushions, the pattern on their plates from their dinner service, patterns round glasses, mugs, and patterned socks. They want to feel they have the autonomy to take their learning where they want to take it. If they didn't bring in things from home they wouldn't get so much out of it and it promotes a learning link between school and home.

(Hen-F-T-S)

The home–school link is another way in which their sense of ownership of their learning places is constructed and cemented, although this is not always the case (Woods *et al.* 1999): 'Marian and I are going on a trip to Knebworth House to look at the Tudors. The children have already started bringing things in, picture art books, dressing up clothes. It gives us the time to say let's get really involved. They engaged with each other more and discussed more and a lot more work came in from home of their own volition' (Cathy, Yr3-T-S). The combination of relevance and ownership is seen through the connection between the home and school projects.

The participants' analysis of why the school had instituted the Grounded in Colour playground project was astute. It also indicated how a sense of place and belonging contributed to ownership:

'Because the teachers wanted us to have fun as well so we can't look out of the window and see other people having fun' (Didea). 'And it's our playground and we should choose some of the things we want for our playground. So when you go out into the playground you can think this was part of something you helped to make' (Emma). 'So we don't feel left out' (Didea). 'I think they want us to be more involved round the school and here the things are mostly the children's choices so when it's finished it's what we want, not somebody else's choice' (Abdul).

(Yr5-T)

Altruism contributed to the sense of place and belonging as the whole school project developed to improve the playground: 'You can learn people's ideas and you can make things for the playground' (Sophia, Yr5-T). Much of the creative learning at Tunnel School was centred on real problems, and this authenticity also heightened a sense of ownership:

'I remember when they told us we were going to make chairs and I thought, "Yes, sure, that's another thing adults say you're going to do and you never do it"' (Usha). 'Making a chair or a seat is one of those hard things you think you'll never be able to do and there's loads of stuff you think is impossible like you never think that when you grow up you'd be an author, it's one of those things that you think is never going to happen' (Freya).

(Yr5-T)

The 'real' projects, such as designing outdoor maths games for younger children in the school, generated a sense of worth about their self/identity: 'I have many ideas like the shapes game and the numbers game and I just thought which would make kids happy and enjoy themselves. I thought of co-ordinates because I know that they will learn and enjoy themselves' (Ryan, Yr6-S). A sense of well-being ensued from the activity, indicative of the development of self-esteem identified by Breakwell (1986) as the third principle of individuality.

Conclusion

Securing learners' ownership of knowledge meant ensuring that their experiences were meaningful to them in terms of their self-identity, characterised by identity play, a sense of achievement, and a sense of place. These identities reflect a career path in which home, playground and school play an integral part but they also reflect the young participants' agency in redefining (Pollard and Filer 1999) their situation and personal identity. The meaningfulness for them is one that involves a visceral experience, a reflective personal one concerned with self-identity 'appropriated by the individual through a process of interaction with others. Only if an identity is confirmed by others is it possible for that identity to be real to the individual holding it. In other words, identity is the product of an interplay of identification and self-identification' (Berger and Luckman 1976, p. 73).

Meaningfulness is therefore also a social phenomenon and the research highlighted the particular nature of that experience through the abundant co-participation that was central to creative learning (Jeffrey 2004). Where efforts have been made by teachers to maintain elements of creative teaching and learning, the sense of ownership has been a social one, both in the construction and appreciation of creative outcomes across time and situations.

The development of knowledge, learning skills and self-confidence of a learner is built on the entire accumulation of a child's previous experiences (Pollard *et al.* 2000). Each of these characteristics is subtle and multi-faceted, requiring empathy, understanding and judgement from teachers. The child in the classroom is working his or her way through a pupil career, is developing physically as well as personally, is engaged in a process of *becoming*. While this is much less tangible to assess than standardised scores, it is no less important. In fact, some argue that there is no accepted definition of understanding for learner achievement and so we should keep records of pupils' feelings, strengths and difficulties (Boostrom 1994). Indeed, the reality is that these two major sets of factors interact together to produce both educational and personal outcomes. Pollard *et al.* (2000) suggest a need for balance between these two objectives. Sustained attention to curricular instruction should be complemented by a provision for the development of pupils' learning skills and self-confidence (ibid., p. 305).

Pupils strive to make sense of learning on their own terms, based on their own interests. In order to achieve this, some argue that learning takes place best when a mutually shared understanding between teachers and pupils is built through negotiative discussion (Woods 1995). Central to meaningful learning is a sharing by teachers of the processes of exploring knowledge and the institution of pedagogy relevant to their experiences and interests. It is this area that needs promoting, if there is to be any development of a learner inclusive (Craft and Jeffrey 2004; Jeffrey and Craft 2004) approach in schools and if learners are going to become complete owners of the knowledge and identities they possess.

4   Innovation

Our fourth characteristic of creative learning is innovation. Creative learning by definition is purposive. In broad terms the product aimed for is change. The learner is changed in some way, most particularly by acquiring new knowledge and new skills, and undergoing personal change. There are transformations in the learner's conceptions, understanding and the uses to which knowledge may be applied. There are also transformations in the learner's understanding of self and identity and of social relations.

The acquisition of new knowledge

A varied array of new knowledge is acquired, internalised and processed through the self. It can be factual knowledge of specific interests, for example space, the rain cycle, the Romans and reproduction, or about specific artefacts, institutions and processes. Although knowledge about such subjects can be gained by teaching methods like rote learning, testing approaches, and reward systems, knowledge gained through creative teaching and learning has particular meaning for the learner. It becomes part of them, adding to the development of the complex self. Further, the knowledge gained will connect to positive emotions of fun, excitement and achievement, ensure an abiding interest in the subject matter and motivate them to engage in further learning in other areas.

One way in which this is done is through bringing subjects alive. An example in our research was by integrating corporeal expression, cognitive engagement and social action to illustrate the 'big bang' theory of the origin of the universe:

> In groups of four in a circle they begin to build their fists on top of one another. They discuss who is to go first and then enjoy the sensation of the explosion after the construction as they throw their fists into the air, smiling and laughing and allowing their bodies to fly away. They then make a ladder of their heads placing them on top of each other ear to ear all facing the same direction. They laugh as the

ladder is constructed and are then full of giggles, screams, shouts and chattering as they sprint away representing the explosion.

(FN-17/10/03-Yr5-V)

Their knowledge of the universe and its operation in the dance project of 'how the earth first got light' becomes imbued in their corporeal engagement: 'It's a giant place, there's no end to it that we know and there's loads of planets' (Issaka). 'They all rotate round each other like we were holding hands and going round in circles' (Gemma). 'The sun has a gravitational pull and everything is round it' (Issaka) (Yr5-V).

Being a comet appeared to have instilled an unforgettable imaginative knowledge of the experience:

'A comet is like a red ball and it has a tail and we had to make it in lines in the hall' (Jordon). 'We had four people joined up together facing one way, standing still and you're all connected' (Nadine). 'The tallest was at the front of the line and at the back of the line was the smallest. We joined together and there were words like jump, turn, twist so whoever was number 1 then number 2, 3, 4 so all the ones go to one place and then we all followed them twisting and turning' (Newton).

(Yr6-V)

This particular project was an extension of a classroom-based project done for an hour a week for five weeks supporting the classroom learning: 'We go to dance because Martin shows us our solar system by movement and we understand what the teacher is telling us about it' (Victoria, Yr5-V).

Cross-curriculum strategies were also particularly effective. 'We did it through lots of different subjects, so it wasn't so boring. Lots of people don't like history because it's boring so if you do it in different subjects it's not' (Reece, Yr5-T). This kind of understanding opens up opportunities to engage learners in constructing the curriculum:

'When you're writing the story you can use your body to explain it, showing the story instead of writing it. You could use dance to show what it was like in Victorian times, how they felt in school or being an orphan, how they worked for money. You could express sadness with your body, by circling round and bringing your arms into your chest and drop them down onto the floor. You could express yourself dying from hunger. You could just move forward and then just slowly stop and die but not abruptly' (Ope). 'Also a scrunch roll, showing that you are sad and you just want to be in one corner' (Sheera).

(Yr5-V)

We see here knowledge about the nature of the subject as well as what it produces. In this way, creative learning is helping to produce scientists – as well as authors, dancers, musicians, etc. This not only secures the optimum learning, but inspires its continuance:

> If you act out a story you find the story interesting. You think about doing some different actions and as you study the character you make up some words to put in the script. I enjoyed it because it makes me excited and I want to read more of it and do more plays and learn more about it, like the Dr. Faustus story. You write down some facts concerning what you want to write about and do a story setting and then write a story about it, something different, but not exactly the same. It just makes you interested in it and makes you creative.
>
> (Anton, Yr5-T)

New knowledge results from the learner being given the freedom to engage with complexity. This leads not only to new knowledge about the subject but reflective knowledge about the processes leading to the knowledge. Thus, knowledge about complexity in patterns in a maths project was matched by the understanding of the complex engagements that make up meaningful learning:

> The pattern I have done on this paper plate with the materials provided is too complicated. I wanted to see how many shapes I could put on it. I've made new shapes and now I have to name them. This one is an oval and this is a triangle. This one starts like an oval but it loops round. There are loads of triangles. If I do one again I think I'll do it differently, simpler, it's too complicated. There are bits coming out of it everywhere. It's been quite hard but enjoyable but I would still enjoy a simpler one. I wouldn't have to attach the bits with sellotape to keep them on. It would still be satisfying but simpler with not so many bits.
>
> (Jamie, Yr2-S)

Although immersed in the technology of the operation, the learner's knowledge of formal shapes becomes almost incidental as the process itself becomes an absorbing activity in which knowledge of the names and properties of shapes will become part of the owned knowledge. Any assumption that learners like things to be simple have been constantly challenged in this research where engaging with complexity is experienced as challenging and motivational, providing the pedagogy is creative: 'The colouring is less important than making a complex pattern' (Alex, Yr3-S).

The subtlety of 'scaffolding' (Bruner 1986) is recognised as effective learning: 'It gets you started off and then you can add your movements to it. It's easier than using your imagination to think of the whole thing. It gives you a head start' (Nicholas, Yr6-H). Such is their understanding of scaffolding that they can be critical when it is not operated properly:

'Sometimes they do it for you. Sometimes they think you can't do something and you can' (Lily). 'We should say to them that we understand now and we want them to leave us alone to do it. If they spot you doing something wrong they should point out that the result is not correct and then leave us to correct it and start telling us all over again how to do it' (Heather). 'If we get one thing wrong they often think we don't understand it all and explain it all over again' (Nicholas).

(Yr5-S)

They appreciate the importance of a 'hands-on' approach: 'You can't imagine what the Tudor fabrics look like until you go and see them, fabrics are different now' (Shabina, Yr5-T). First-hand investigations are central to transforming learning and seen as a major insight into effective learning: 'What I liked was that you actually get to see the wildlife and we looked at this reed boat that they had actually made and there was this bird park where you could actually look at the birds' (Emma, Yr6-T). This hands-on approach challenged stereotypes from the media:

When we went to Hampton Court we found the other side of the story really. We believed in one thing and it was not totally true. We thought that he [Henry VIII] just picked up his food like chicken legs and chucked it behind him. All the things that you've been told or you believe is rubbish. You have to wipe that out and listen to what they've got to say.

(Martin, Yr6-G)

Young participants' interest in authentic knowledge is paramount: 'I'd prefer not to know a load of lies like different stories. I'd like to know the real thing that happened' (Jamie, Yr6-G). These perceptions show that the pupils have understood many of the intentions of their teacher concerning the importance of evidence, but also they show that they have taken up an interest in history.

Insights into the power of creative learning are provided by 'real projects' – those that contributed to classroom, school, community or global life: 'The playground shelters project is getting children involved so it's not just designing something and then forgetting about it, it's getting them involved so they can't be lazy about it. And if they're involved they might remember and do something for their children when they're older' (Didier, Yr5-T).

Finding out something new is a joyful experience. We saw this in a variety of activities including the construction of large geo-domes, the making and marketing of pizzas, designing adventure playgrounds in a design and technology week, work on the moral aspects of temptation through the Faustus drama project, the design and construction of seating for a school playground, the design of 3D maths games for the same playground and the exploration of sounds in the environment.

For creative teachers:

> You have to open up possibilities, to nurture the joy of learning, it sounds a bit fanciful but it does, because if you're inspired it motivates many children. Joy of learning is awe and wonder, 99 per cent or 100 per cent captivated audience, time rushes by and lesson finished, that's the joy of learning, and when they come to you the next day, 'Mrs C., we did this, I've found this in a book', you know you've started something, that's the joy of learning.
>
> (Tess, Yr5-T-S)

In the dance project, focusing on the beginning of the universe, the participants were being guided through an exploration of physical possibilities and compositions orchestrated by the dance teachers but there was a feeling that 'you can do real body movement dancing, you can really free your body. You feel you're having a good time and stuff' (Jordon). They were freed from being a pupil, free to 'be outrageous and work with partners and friends without the teacher putting you in a group and at the same time you never had to be left out' (Abibola). They experienced and celebrated a physical freedom from within: 'I've learnt about how you can free your body when you put your arms out and stretch your finger tips' (Kalvin); a kind of 'floating. We had to do it in order so we were turning round like we were floating' (Victoria). They relished the opportunities to 'experiment with your body, to do things that you've never done before' (Yan). These freedoms led to avenues for emotional expression with peers, 'I like doing different shapes because if you're angry with someone but you don't want to express it in a way that's obvious, you can express it differently' (Lottie), and for oneself: 'letting yourself go out, like if you're angry you can just do it and let out how you're feeling inside' (Shimona); 'I like it because if you're angry all you have to do is put your anger out, through dancing' (Sheera) (Yrs5+6-V).

This freedom also involved taking the body out of the self and into new realms of personification as a vicarious experience: 'You actually felt like a planet. I asked myself "where shall I go next in the solar system?" It was exciting, an interaction between people and planets, all of us were turning into each other' (Issaka, Yr5-V).

The pleasure gained from freeing the body was accompanied by a dynamism in which all the gestures, turns, leaps, shuffles, strides, waves, stretches, touches and swirls were dynamic movements generating tautness, strength and flowing expressions. They were vigorous: 'I think I enjoyed the creation most because I like learning about different cultures in history. I liked the spider and doing the wings and the cutting action' (Issaka). 'I enjoyed it when we ran into our comets and then ran out because I like running a lot and I like making actions' (Kalvin). 'When you run about you're active and you release your energy' (Yan) (Yr6-H).

Teachers exploited the joy that came from the visceral whenever possible. The Faustus drama project was a series of ten workshops over two terms concerned with the themes in the play, such as temptation, and the other aspects of drama, such as music, movement, character, puppet performance, set design and drama construction. The workshops encouraged a great deal of creative expression and interaction of a number of story plots which meant a great deal of playing different characters:

> Kate reminds them about a story that they know, Orpheus and the underworld. She then tells them two more stories, the first is an Indian story about a princess called Savitri who has to persuade an evil kidnapper to give up her future husband and the second is the story of Persephone.
>
> The children are then divided into three groups and they have to pick a scene from their story and show it as a tableau to represent the whole story. One person narrates the story and characters come to the front occasionally and then return to their place. One child asks if the narrators can move around.
>
> As they talk in the groups about the composition of the story their hands wave in the air and they jump excitedly. They point, call one another, take a position or pose with one another; they cajole, suggest, wave their arms, spring, threaten in role, purloin a chair, enjoin their bodies, wrap themselves around each other and squeal. They mimic screams, push people into position, watch, wait, listen, frown, persuade, experiment in groups, compose in different groups, argue, insist, shunt, volunteer, propose, and look perplexed.
>
> (FN-25/11/03-T)

Creative learning has an emotional heart resulting in flows of energy (Woods and Jeffrey 1996) and the seeking of pleasure (Emilia 1996). This is illustrated in the detailed descriptions of their work, in this case a model of an adventure playground constructed by a six-year-old:

> I made the slide. You go up there, through the hole and down the slide. This is a lamp post made from pipe cleaners and we both did the sand pit together. We put in a bucket. There are some flowers and a bench made out of matchsticks. And I have put a very steep slide on it. I got some matchsticks on paper and made a roundabout. I did some knots to keep the material on the slide tower on. This is a monkey bar slide. You can climb on the second swing across and let go into the sand pit. We used the matchsticks stuck into the ground to make little areas to play in. I liked doing the swirly, whirly bit of the slide because it was quite fiddly and I like doing fiddly things. You have to hold them and play with it a lot. When you pull the whirly slide the little girl on the high bridge wobbles. She's on high bar above the ground balancing on

the bridge. We've put steps up to the slide. I've learnt how to model things and to really make things and to make things wobble without touching them. I learnt how to take things and make them into something they really are not.

(Amy, Yr1-S)

The joy of learning is bound up with the opportunity to use imagination and to play with materials, situations or, in this case, words:

> I observed a planning session on how to market the pizzas they had designed and made. I also observed them eating them. 'I never knew melted chocolate would taste so good on melted cheese' (Tom). 'I never usually have ham and it's lovely' (Laurie). 'I don't like pizzas, only the ones I make. I don't like all the tomato on it but I made my own and put on only a little' (Emil). 'A scrumptious, delumptious, cheeky, cheesey, honey, dummy, yummy, pizza' (Kay).
>
> (FN-14/07/04-Yr3-S)

The search for peak experience produced integrity of process:

> The children are learning how to work in a circle, going in and out and circling round in different directions. Their faces are serious as they have to concentrate on the beat and the direction of turn when the circle goes round in the opposite direction. They are learning about unity and unison in the universe. As they practise their universe 'birth and sound' sequence they watch the leader with a studied intent as they perform the flash jump, the smooth roll, the scrunch roll and the flame leap. Their eyes follow their arms looking into space with slow stretched turns. Nadine smiles as she explodes and follows this with a spiky roll and a swirl.
>
> (FN-21/11/03-V)

The acquisition of new meaningful knowledge is self-perpetuating. It contains its own motivation. The absorption of meaningful knowledge is to want to follow wherever it takes you, to follow your new interest and passion. History through creative learning 'made me want to come to school. Now we've done the Tudors and the acting I want to come to school' (Freya, Yr5-T). It's

> made me want to read more about the Tudors. It's like reading a book and you're on a tense bit and you want to read more. I would like to know more about how the plague was stopped and how they changed things. Why everything now is not the same as then. What happened to change our lives? Now we've got computers and we've got cars and they didn't have those things. If the Tudors hadn't had a war with the Spanish

it might have been different today, there might not have been a Civil War in the USA or World War 2 and we might not have been born.

(Reece, Yr5-T)

Knowledge is not confined to the facts of a subject of focus. It may include ethical elements that are part of the objectives of the investigation as in the study of the Tudor play about Faustus. Learners in this project learned a lot about persuasion, temptation, good and evil and these were made more meaningful by the dramatic activity in which they engaged, leaving them with an experience of loss and purgatory: 'I would still have turned down the offer from the devil because it wasn't worth it. It's about killing people and not trusting the evil. Not to be greedy otherwise you might be punished. It's about not trusting the devil. If there was Heaven and Hell you would know the right thing to do' (Zizzi, Yr5-T).

The use of drama and music stimulates interest in subjects such as history. 'I would like to learn about the cavemen times. I'd like to learn how they got their food, how they made their weapons, how they got there, how did the world begin and how did people form, 'cos no-one would really know the truth about how people formed, no-one knows. The thing about Adam and Eve could just be a big fairy tale' (John, Yr6-G). Their cognitive development also concerns social issues:

The children have been encouraged to think about the symbolism of objects placed within portraits. 'The hearts in our picture of Catherine of Aragon represents her broken heart and her marriage. One is red and one is black. We put necklaces in because she had them in the original picture we looked at and we have put sequins in to make it more detailed. We did the background black because we thought it looked better than the original brown. She was his first wife and she was divorced. His wives were divorced, beheaded, died, divorced, beheaded, survived. The third Queen had a boy called Edward. Henry wanted lots of wives because he wanted to be famous and very rich' (Sophie). 'He wanted a boy because he would get on with a boy' (Megan). 'He couldn't trust a girl' (Sophie). 'Tudors thought that women were weaker than men' (Zizzi). 'People believed that men would be better and that women would be weaker' (Megan). 'They believed that in war women would not be strong enough and would not be able to cope' (Zizzi).

(Yr5-S)

For both girls and boys this was meaningful learning about the nature of their own gender and of how power operated in gender relations. Similarly, creative learning involves acquiring knowledge about teaching and learning. 'Martin [the dance teacher] is working very hard at trying to get us to get down to business. He is trying his hardest to make sure we do it in the time he's got so that when we do the dance we have remembered by heart' (Martin, Yr6-V). These insights provide criteria for assessing good teaching: 'What I like about Martin is that he doesn't give up when people can't do it, either he goes over there and helps or he gets someone who knows how to do it to help' (Maryanne, Yr5-V).

Creative learning encourages an understanding of learning to learn (Black *et al.* 2006):

> 'Learning is learning how. It includes failure and practice and thinking, strategies, different skills and different ways of doing things. We need to think about what we are trying to do. We are conscious of something in our minds' (Alex). 'Learning is a step towards something. I am learning that you make mistakes and then practise' (Jake). 'Learning involves planning, like experimenting and being briefed first. It's experimenting, testing, and finding out for ourselves' (Carl). 'It's becoming your own teacher, teaching yourself, choosing the way you want to do it. Choosing is important because you choose the best way of doing it. You know yourself better than others. You can choose your own level, less challenging and more challenging' (Patrick).
>
> (Yr5-S)

The comments above, gained in a few minutes' conversation with a group of learners, summarises creative learning as relevant to the individual (knowing yourself), consisting of a significant amount of control (to use imagination and thinking skills), ownership (becoming your own teacher) and innovation ('a step toward something').

The acquisition of new skills

Creative learning promotes a wide variety of skills. There are skills of experimentation and speculation, of possibility thinking, of discernment and risk taking, and the ability to develop links and connections to anticipate, sustain and technically manipulate resources, ideas and concepts. There are social skills of learning. There are also transferable skills that learners are able to use in different learning situations, across subjects and socially. We discuss some of the more prominent of these.

Cognitive skills

Cognitive skills in creative learning include creative thinking, one of the set of thinking skills identified by the National Curriculum. This has been characterised as tearing up and building (Beetlestone 1998), as imagining, investigating, anticipating, organising and controlling of ideas and judgements (Halliwell 1993), collaborations (Cocklin *et al.* 1999), associative collaboration with peers (Dowrick 1993), playing with ideas, possibilities and evaluations (NACCCE 1999), and the freedom to investigate, make mistakes and to choose (Emilia 1996).

After periods of creative learning, learners are 'more able to try out new ideas, they're more able to take risks in terms of dance. I can see a clear difference between the choices they're making now, and the choices they made in that first week' (Dance teacher-H). They learn how to 'watch each other and come up with something interesting to say about what they'd seen. And I think their observation skills are getting much better. They are more discerning' (ibid.). They learn the skill of experimentation: 'You get a lot of ideas from other people and you can try out all of them and see which ones suit that dance better' (Miles, Yr6-H).

They learn to speculate:

> I asked some children who were working on a design and technology project focusing on food, 'Should all lessons have something to do with eating?' Their ideas were wide ranging and innovative: 'We could eat what they ate in the past.' 'We could drink the blood.' 'We could do sums with sweets.' 'We could eat the plants we draw in art.' 'We could sing while we were eating.' 'We can experiment with different ways of cooking a potato for science.' 'We could describe different sweets for literacy.' 'We could make potato letters and print them.' 'We could have a tray of Smarties and use them in maths.' 'We could print out pictures on edible paper.'
>
> (Yr4-S)

Technical skills

Technical skill refers to the manipulation of resources, ideas and concepts and the learner's ability to anticipate demands and consequences, to sustain engagement: 'For me that manipulation, giving them lots of vocabulary in the warm-up work, giving them the opportunity to manipulate a sequence, was a confidence builder. They knew more of what to expect and it also gave them some tools to use in their own creativity, sustain something, to concentrate more to work effectively in a group' (Dance teacher-H). 'Glen tells me that a number of boys – Gareth, Ishmael, David and Ewen – didn't initially want to do the dancing but that they have been converted. Amy and Nina read out their poetry for the first time recently and he put this down to the confidence they have gained in the dance project and all the girls are taking more part in answering questions' (FN-25/02/04-Yr6-T-H).

Technical skills gained through creative learning are those which entail some feature of operation, risk taking, experimentation and problem solving. Those gained through instrumental instruction involve no development of the skill, only the repetitive reproduction of the artefact, movement or plan. The skills are relevant to the creative learner for they develop them as they use them and use them to develop their projects. This encourages more experimentation for development and perfection and the ownership of the skills maintains the motivation to seek new methods to improve their skills further. The technical skills gained from 'hands on' activities are part of the necessary technical skills needed for life:

> These Yr5 learners are in the process of a week's work on designing and constructing containers via a history topic on the Aztecs. I asked them what they had learnt. 'It is how to design something and not mess it up, to reduce the failure rate and to make a box with tabs.' 'We learnt scoring and cutting skills, how to draw accurately, improve computation skills, folding skills, manipulate scissors and to measure.'
>
> (FN-20/05/03-S)

Technical skills are nurtured through 'hands on' and 'real projects' such as the playground seats. Sam, the project artist, asks technical questions and they come up with solutions: 'we could have double sided sticky tape', 'we will have a sponge so that people won't get hurt', 'we will use a sliding door' (FN-20/09/04-Yr6-T). These skills are grasped by the very young as well as older learners:

> I am with the Foundation class (aged 5) in the ICT suite. They are working in threes producing a firework in the software program Dazzle. 'We don't want some white' (Neve). 'We can go over it' (Melissa), 'with red' (Azone). 'I'll throw it away and now I'll put it back. It won't go' (Melissa). 'I'll do another. Your turn, Azone' (Neve). 'Your turn, Melissa' (Azone). 'I'll put it back for you – there' (Neve). 'You're making the whole page go pink' (Azone). 'I'll get it back' (Melissa). 'Let's have some blue on it' (Azone). 'Try to use the same colour with different shades' (Teacher). 'We could do another' (Azone), 'with different colours' (Neve). They keep dumping them and starting again. 'I'll put it into the bin. I want to kiss it goodbye' (Melissa).
>
> (FN-22/05/03-S)

Young learners are quick to use their technical skills to solve specific problems but they also learn patience and determination:

> Daniel, Joshua and Rebecca are constructing their adventure playgrounds from junk material. They had visited an adventure playground as part of the design and technology week. 'I did this roundabout and a see-saw, and a slide. Underneath there is a sand pit and we cut out the straws for the sand. It took us two days to complete it. It's very exciting because you help one another if they can't do something' (Joshua).
>
> (FN-16/07/03-F-S)

Presentation skills also feature in creative learning projects, particularly where control and ownership are central:

> It's good that my project presentation includes a diagram. You need a picture for the labels on the tiger that describe parts of its body. It is helpful to have a 'did you know facts' because it might inspire the person who is reading it more. It makes the page more interesting to read.
>
> (Hamish, Yr5-T)

Social skills

Participative engagements are unavoidable in creative classrooms and collaboration is encouraged. Learners develop their own collaborative skills in creative learning contexts:

> The children work in small groups to compose a greeting composition as part of this confidence building project. They are seen concentrating, negotiating, watching each other in groups, listening, experimenting, proposing, considering, rejecting, evaluating, being serious with faint smiles, engaging, following, leading, agreeing, contrasting, expressing, trying – all focused. Two groups join together to share a composition and do it together and construct a sequence and final tableau for the audience. These composition sessions are where they are most focused, the pictures show them fully engaged, cognitively as well as collaboratively.
>
> (FN-25/02/04-Yr6-H)

Co-participative skills are enhanced in a creative learning situation where learners are encouraged to use each other as a resource: 'I pick out their ideas and I express it in a different way and change it a bit and then I use it again, so it's like copying it' (Corin, Yr5-V). This reverses a dominant ethos in other learning contexts where copying is often frowned upon. Here it is part of learning – it does have an educational purpose used in a certain way. Leadership skills are also enhanced:

> Carly's class are divided into soup companies. There are five people in each group with a manager and a director who picks a team to ensure a good standard and quality of product. They have to draw a product and construct it. They have to collaborate and communicate. They have to make the soup, advertise it, construct a slogan, put ingredients on the package, design the tin, and decide on the price. They have to bring in £2 to pay for the ingredients. Some possibilities are chicken and mushroom, chilli and tomato sauce. They have to prepare a company sign and a new logo. Some of the suggestions were 'Food fanatics', 'Food dudes', 'The crazy team', 'Srano', 'The cotter caters'. In one team Katie, a learner, is collecting their wrapper designs and collating them,

taking one item from each design and using it in an overall design. She is doing this because she is the neatest person in the group.

(FN-15/07/03-Yr4-S)

By speaking and listening to others the flow of action constructs and builds a sense of self by providing terms to individuals they may employ when talking about themselves to others (Pennuel and Wertsch 1995). The construction of a creative vocabulary in the classroom (Jeffrey 2004) provided opportunities for learners to inhabit and appropriate the discourse. It seeped into everyday conversation just as it would in a community of artists:

> I talk to a group of girls during their reading session, Nadia, Julia and Nidha. 'Reading stories is about using my imagination and creativity.' 'Creativity is about our texture and creating things and sculpting.' 'It's mainly about art and colours and creating from the imagination.' 'We argue when we work together but we also put our minds together to make a creative thing.' 'If we were talking to younger children about reading we would ask them for details of the character.'
>
> (FN-12/11/03-T)

The skills of participative learning derive from creative projects:

> 'I liked working together with all of us doing different things.' 'I like watching the other crew and laughing.' 'We agreed things by changing it as we discussed it.' 'If you belong to a team you feel you are being listened to. It's good to have others caring about your ideas.' 'We have learnt how to co-operate and how to use tools and how to be creative with vegetable leftovers and to make pictures.'
>
> (Yr4-S)

Many schools that commit to creative learning also have school councils for primary children representing ages 7–11 (Fielding 2007). These model democracy and inclusion in some decision-making activities and young participants gain worthy committee and negotiative skills as they take part.

> Last thing in the afternoon I attended the School's Council and recorded it. Apart from me, the head teacher was the only other adult present and one of the children chaired the meeting. The agenda was specifically about the playground and the cage during break and lunchtimes. They suggested that there should be opportunities for other games such as basketball and that there was too much football. Someone suggested they could use the cage for half the week for football and the other half for basketball. They asked for a running track and the chairperson suggested using the disco money to buy equipment. The group was reminded that bad language in the playground is dealt

with by letters from the School's Council and the head teacher to the individual and their parents.

The meeting was taken seriously and there was no problem with different ages. A boy had brought a laptop to take notes but the head took them as well. They suggested coloured codes on balls for different classes and giving their 'peer supporters' a greater role in sorting out problems. (These are children nominated across the key stage 2 and act to ameliorate conflict and distress in the playground. They attend courses and are trained to do this.) Lastly, one child asked the head teacher how much money does the school have and she promised to bring the budget to the next meeting. The ideas will go to the staff and are brought back to the council in the New Year.

(FN-11/12/04-T)

Skilled social relations result from creative learning projects such as the Faustus story and Tudor times: 'Drama helped me get on with new people. It made making friends easier. Maybe I've become better at it' (Mickey, Yr5-T).

Personal development

Creative learning can lead to moments or periods of profound insight, which in turn leads to new knowledge of the self and radical self-development. In the early 1990s, we noted such experiences in what we called 'critical events' – critical in the sense of being highly significant, representing catalytic effect and uncommon advance – in the educational careers of those involved (Woods 1993). One such event was the 'Rushavenn' project, which involved a group of primary pupils working with their teacher and a well-known children's author over a period of a year to produce a children's book (Whistler 1988). This won high praise from literary experts. It was also a considerable educational accomplishment. Thus, the pupils involved all claimed considerable personal development involving a great increase in confidence; a willingness to talk and to risk expression of ideas; heightened motivation; a growth in sense of self-worth and self-esteem; a feeling of control of the learning process; a sense of achievement, thrill and pride in a job well done; and a record of which had been preserved for posterity. They also spoke of refinement of their learning skills – improved reading and writing, literary appreciation, the formulation and expression of ideas, and insight into the artist's mind and the act of creation. These students had a remarkable ability to situate the event within their school career. It gave a perspective to things that had happened since, and provided a sharp awareness of alienative processes. The students themselves (now teenagers by the time the research was conducted) attested to this. Stephen, for example, looking back, said it gave him confidence to write, whereas before confidence was, like maths, number crunching. You had to be given a task and you had to do it, and the teacher would look at the spelling, that sort of thing … It taught me that's not what writing was about at all. There's no point in writing something down if you're not going to mean what you say … You've got to feel inside that you're telling the truth.

(Woods 1993, p. 16)

The idea of the book, however, was more subtle than just to make you an author. Stephen thought

it was to expand you as a person, as an individual, not just in areas of writing and illustrations and that sort of thing. If that's what it set out to do, then it's achieved its goal, because that set me off realising that there was more to life than just a teacher imparting knowledge upon you in terms of education.

(ibid., p. 17)

Sarah found the project gave her

a lot of confidence, speaking in a group and telling people my ideas, and it gave me probably confidence with the work I was doing. It made me feel that my pieces of paper weren't inferior to anybody else's. It made me feel it was worthwhile trying to do my best.

(ibid., p. 17)

Our more recent research project provides more examples. Insights into learners' own self-identity came from creative learning, and are shared, critiqued and appreciated:

'The dramatic approach to learning has made my memory better. I can go into a different personality. Sometimes with friends I can shift into different personalities. I have done so because sometimes people don't believe me and it makes me more believable. I have a store of different personalities in my brain that I choose to be' (Micky). 'He likes it because it gets people's attention. Maybe he wasn't getting enough attention' (Hamish). 'I like people laughing when I say something funny. I improvise to try and make it funny because they are enjoying it more and because they're laughing, it makes you happier' (Frankie).

(Yr5-T)

Insights into the effect the subject, in this case dance, can have on one's well-being arises from creative learning: 'If you're angry you can just do it and show how you're feeling inside' (Shimona). 'I like it because if you're angry all you have to do is to put your anger out, through dancing' (Sheera) (Yr5-V).

There is often an 'Aha!' factor (Jackson 1992) in which a learner, or a group of learners, suddenly realises the quality of a subject under investigation, a process or a realisation of the subjective connection between the learning experience and their self-identity:

> I think it was when Jordon was working on that duet with Ash on the beginning of the earth. It was almost like he had an overall sense of what this thing was, and he took Ash with him. When you look at him you think he wouldn't say boo to a goose but he seemed to have a really good choreographic understanding of what would be interesting.
>
> (Dance teacher, Yr5-V)

Projects were not just about learning new knowledge creatively but about developing the young participants' identity, character and self-esteem:

> I think there has been a much wider range of outcomes than if I had just said 'now we are going to learn about the Tudors x, y and z' because there was so much personal and social development going on as well. There were children who were very quiet in class and they really came out of their shells. The outdoor projects were just a vehicle for that social and personal development. Tolerance, patience, appreciating everybody's efforts, not comparing them, not ranking them, but appreciating how everybody came together for the performance at the end and how everybody valued everybody's efforts.
>
> (Graham, Yr5-DH-T)

Insights into the value of good social relations for effective learning also emerge from creative learning. You learn new things about other people, and about yourself in your reactions to them:

> You might think someone is really horrible but then you work with them and you find out that they're really nice and you can play with them and it affects them as well because then they do their work and they're not always worrying that they don't have any friends.
>
> (Iris, Yr5-T)

Creative learning adds insights into positive relations: 'They might learn something from the other person if they're not so good. If you share ideas you are being helpful and you are making them feel proud of themselves. You're making them happy and you are proud of what you have taught them' (Maryanne, Yr5-H). Sociability is recognised as motivating learners: 'I enjoy all of it, not just that you are happy and crack jokes with other people, it's because it makes us want to carry on doing the dance as well, so you go for a couple of weeks and you want to carry on' (Miles, Yr6-H). Creative learning was smiling (Amandeep), being friendly (Emma), being co-operative (Didier) and helping one another (Emma) (Yr5-T).

Social learning needs its own language to enable young participants to talk about themselves and their learning (Kane and Maw 2005), just one of the 100 languages of children (Emilia 1996). It creates warmth and the satisfaction that comes with recognising a collective humanity:

'This piece of masking tape is to separate the sand pit and a slide from the football pitch. We used a pipe cleaner to make the entrance to the football pitch.' 'I put some shiny paper on the football pitch so it looks like the proper one. My partner thought it was a good idea.' 'Some slides have sand at the bottom so we put some masking tape there.' 'You have got to work with a partner and do lots of things that are in a real park.' 'I have learnt to share with one another and to give one another time to finish things.' 'I would get my young brother to do something simple that they have done at the nursery.' 'It's been a little difficult to make the rocket because it's so big. She's doing the best she can. I am getting the base ready. I'm nearly ready, just two more holes to do.'

(FN-16/07/03-Yr1-S)

Social learning is cohesive, for young participants are emotional and cultural beings (Woods and Jeffrey 1996):

The children are thinking how to make it stronger, their faces look happy because they're working together, there's a special bond, when you work together you become better friends, you're learning with somebody else. Yes, because they've tried really hard with each other and he's learnt with Hamish different ways of sticking a head on.

(Joe, Yr5-T)

The teamwork Graham talks about is one that is imbued with consideration for others:

I think it's a great thing that all ideas were listened to. No idea was dismissed out of hand. Children adopted the idea that all ideas were good and you needed to listen to them and if you've got a good idea you listened to someone else's idea and then you can combine the two to make them even better. They won't dismiss ideas out of hand now whereas before some learners would have done so in the past. Certainly, for the seat design project, they saw that all ideas should be valued, should be considered and paid that respect.

(DH, Yr5-T)

These young participants recognised the value of life history due to a creative learning project on the Second World War. 'Some of our grandparents were in it, some shared the experience about the war and some people were, like, talking about themselves' (Valma). 'Yes, that's true; some people like to share their stuff 'cos they like talking about themselves' (Amandeep) (Yr5-T).

Social learning is both the source of creative learning and a result of it: 'People encourage you to do it and then you say I've just got to do it and you say I'm here now, I can't let down my team even if I'm scared 'cos I would let down my team and people encourage you and say go on, do it' (Anton). 'The first time you don't want to do it and you are on the stage in front of clever people and you are so nervous you might forget the words but my friends encourage me to do it' (Steven). The benefits are social and personal: 'I have learnt to take more advice from others, to encourage me to take part in a play and to help me work on the stage' (Frankie). 'I valued the creativity and being able to talk more clearly to people' (Colette). Social development is aided by those learning media that are rooted in social relations and at the same time they are a vehicle for creative learning: 'Drama helped me get on with new people. It made making friends easier. Maybe I've become better at it. It makes me happy after it because it has filled up a space in my body and they cheer and it feels nice. You get to understand more about each other. We work together and sometimes we talk together and you understand each other better' (Martin) (Yr5-T). The transformation of social relations for those engaged in creative learning is an experience of equality, status, well-being, warmth towards one's peers and significant others and a commitment to engage more often in social learning for the good it does its participants.

Creative learning employs and enhances the whole of the learner. This includes the area of feelings and emotions. In fact feelings are very important, not only as a product to aim for, in their refinement, but as an aid in promoting innovation generally:

> When we do it in drama we put physical actions with the words to rein-force their meaning; even if you don't understand all the words you feel you know the emotions behind it and the feelings behind them. This morning I think there were some children who didn't know what the words were about but Kate was putting that kinaesthetic angle on it; this is how you would be feeling if you were saying these words. I think that's great, I think that's one way you can get across English words. I think it would be difficult to get across the meaning of these words just by reading these words – good and evil – and discussing them. The physical activities that go along with them reinforce that learning.
>
> (Graham, Yr5-T-T)

Empathy is a vital aspect of gaining meaningful knowledge for it appeals directly to the emotions involved in teaching and learning and to the human ability to imagine life and experience from other perspectives (Woods and Jeffrey 1996). The identification with a subject matter and immersion of the self into that subject – in this case the beginning of the universe – becomes meaningful:

'I really liked it because it's like you're the actual planet or the sun or if you're the earth you are going round the sun' (Ash). 'You've got to imagine that you're in space, you actually felt like a planet. I was just like, well where shall I go next in the solar system, it's exciting and interactive. Between people and planets, all of us were turning into each other' (Issaka).

(Yr6-V)

Just as dance was used to mediate knowledge of the solar system, so drama was used to learn about Victorian times and the knowledge gained became embedded in the learner's experience. The tension and conflict in the situation had a lasting effect:

'We dressed up as characters from the street as Victorian schoolgirls and we were frightened of the teachers who had canes. We had a time-line throughout the school and we dressed up and put out pictures on the timeline. It was like a play that week. We found out what it was like being in those times. I didn't know it was so cruel. We had to have a nail check and someone got sent out for wearing red tights and I was sent out because I was a Hindu.' 'It was exciting and scary and it made you think about what it was like. Exciting and scary makes you think about it more. It sticks in your head more.'

(Yr4-T)

Drama representations can become emotionally charged. One confident singer was 'overcome by the sadness of his song' in a play about Tudor times and, during his solo, tears began to roll down his face. His role partner, Nicole, described her feelings as he kept the song going, willed on by a mesmerised audience:

I was tense. I was watching him and thinking, 'Come on Wayne, come on Wayne!' I thought he was going to run out of the hall. I felt really sorry for him. I felt like I was going to cry, too, for him. I was just saying, 'Come on Wayne, you can do it!' I felt like saying that, but I kept quiet and just kept thinking, 'Come on Wayne!' As I walked him back (after his song), I said, 'Are you all right?' and he replied 'Yes'. I said, 'You were really good', and he went 'Thanks'.

(FN-23/04/93-G)

Role play developed the self and identity:

As we were coming down to the hall, all dressed up, I felt like I was a Tudor person. The way we had to walk made me feel like I was a Tudor person. When we were coming out of the hall, having done it, I still felt like a Tudor person. Everyone was looking at me as a Tudor person.

When we got back into the classroom, I took all my clothes off and left on the ones I had underneath, and it felt like I wasn't a Tudor no more. It just felt like I was me. I liked playing both parts, but when I was a Tudor person I missed being me, and when I'm me, I miss being a Tudor person.

(Nicole, Yr6-G)

The design and construction of a covered playground seat, which was actually built with the help of the young participants by the project art facilitator from the girls' designs, enhanced their learning identities: 'I like working hard because at the end you or someone else is going to be proud of me. I think it's a nice feeling to have someone say "that's really nice, you tackled that really well, you found that hard but you still did it"' (Freya, Yr5-T).

Excitement encourages creativity:

I made up some words to put in the script and I enjoy it because it makes me excited and I want to read more of it and do more plays and learn more about it. Doing the Faustus drama felt like you was reading a book and then you said, 'oh, this is very interesting, I might do a play about it', and then you just create anything you want and you read a different story and you write down some couple of facts that you want to write about it and do a story setting and then just write a story about it, something different, but not exactly the same. It just makes you interested about it and just makes you creative.

(Anton, Yr5-T)

Conclusion

The innovation resulting from creative learning is the development of the learners' understanding of curriculum, pedagogy and social learning, the acquisition of meaningful knowledge and new skills with which to engage in learning. The transformation is to their attitude and relationship to learning in schools and to the development of motivated lifelong learners. Knowledge that is owned is remembered – not for a short space of time as for a test or examination, but for years, possibly a lifetime. It has become part of the person. One of our creative schools had an Ofsted inspection during the research period, and the inspectors were astonished at the levels of retention shown by the pupils. The head teacher commented:

Most of the lessons came out as outstanding and all the comments that were fed back to me were, 'the children just know what they're learning about'. They know, all the teachers keep saying, and it's linked to this and because we're doing this and the children are putting up their hands and saying, 'what about this we learned last week, can't we put that in there?' When they spoke to them, she said, 'the children in Yr6 remembered what they'd learned in Yr2'. She said, 'the books they used in literacy, the numeracy activities they did, that type of learning and the retention of learning was phenomenal, really, absolutely phenomenal'.

(Dawn, HT-HA)

Transformations from a social perspective are transformations in the subjectivities of learners and their relations to their practice and the social situation they inhabit in schools (Woods 1993, p. 25). These subjectivities are how they feel about their learning, their labour, the human relations they experience and develop as they experience creative learning. These characteristics apply to the creative learning act, to the learners' experience of the act or event and to the foci we use to research creative learning. A radical shift is indicated, as opposed to more gradual, cumulative learning, with which it is complementary (Woods 2002). In our terms the innovation is defined as an experience of change; creativity is experienced as subjective. If there is no subjective reaction then there is no creative learning. The transformation of social relations for those engaged in creative learning is an experience of equality, status, well-being, warmth towards one's peers and significant others and a commitment to engage more often in social learning for the good it does its participants.

This part has analysed the nature of creative learning through intensive examination of learning experiences, but as we indicated in the introduction, creative teachers' pedagogies have undergone a difficult time in the period since the introduction of the reforms of 1989. We now provide some case studies of how teachers organise creative teaching and how they manage to maintain it.

Part II
Creating opportunities for creative learning

This part includes a number of case studies illustrating the ways in which schools and teachers are providing the contexts for and developing creative learning. The case studies involve special education, inter-school relationships, policy manipulations, a successful arts approach to learning and how schools are taking advantage of the current creativity discourse to push back the domination of the performativity discourse.

5 Achieving breakthroughs in learning

Students as critical others

At its best, creative teaching produces 'breakthroughs' in learning (Woods 1994). They are the ultimate in innovation. Breakthroughs have unusual power to provide startling insights and enlightenment. They cast a brilliant light on the here and now, and reveal startling new truths. There is a sense of ultimates and frontiers. There is new self-knowledge and self-development, significant advances in relationships with others. They are accompanied by profound feelings, great excitement, disturbed emotions, intense pleasure and sometimes pain. They liberate, endowing the learner with freedom from the chains of alienated ignorance and more freedom towards achieving one's goals. They provide resource, not only for oneself, but in one's relationships with others. In short, they are empowering both of the self, and through the self, of others.

We shall concentrate in this chapter on one feature of breakthroughs that seems to have had little publicity as yet, but which is likely to be of increasing significance. We refer to students acting as 'critical others'.

Students as critical others

We have discussed elsewhere the part played by the critical other in enhancing the role of the teacher (Woods 1993). They do this through the provision of a charismatic quality, which because of the pressures they are under it is sometimes difficult for teachers to generate themselves. Critical others (non-teachers who possess a particular specialism that contributes to teaching from time to time) derive their charisma from three main sources: 1. The fact of being other. They challenge the taken-for-granted, introduce novelty, present new role-models for students. 2. Personal qualities emerging from self, providing trust, faith and inspiration, contributing to the strong group feeling and the motivation of individuals. 3. Qualities emerging from 'profession', contributing to the authenticity of teachers' work through the provision of verisimilitude (living history with real archaeologists, designing a real building with architects and planners), and validating teachers' and pupils' work as genuine endeavours. Critical others can play a key role in creative learning.

We want to consider here the role of students as critical others, and the part they play in creative learning. In one example, a number of primary schools were involved in a project on 'global education'. This entailed link-ups through email with children in other schools, both in the UK and other countries. The teacher's evaluation (Camsey 1989, in Woods 1994, p. 135) records:

> The quality of the written work – in both depth of thought and structure – has shown dramatic improvement. Writing for a real audience that actually responds, asks further questions, argues, shares your interests, is the same age and is generally interested in what you have to say achieves more in a matter of weeks than the most skilled and talented teacher can achieve in months. The desire to make sure that what is written has meanings, and is correctly written, results in work of a very high standard being produced.

We have seen some other examples already in the book (see especially Chapter 4). Here, we draw on two case studies from our earlier research to show the power and efficacy of this resource in a little more detail. These are just as relevant now as they were then.

Case Study 1: A residential trip

The first case study conducted in 1989–91 looked at the relationships between two groups of pupils, one group of which had special needs. Robert was the head of a Midlands rural primary school who had been running a programme of semi-integration with a class at a nearby special school for several years. Each year the programme was enlivened by a critical event, culminating in a celebration, such as a play, an exhibition, a film or a field trip. He was concerned about 'the basic continuity of the learning process'. Field weeks were 'a regular commitment, and colour so much of what happens either side of it, so we find it easier to integrate the whole thing into the general curriculum of the school'.

We monitored a two-year period of association between two classes, one consisting of children with special needs (George Ross School). The special needs children visited the other school (Bradfield) for one day per week. They spent their time partly on basic, standard tasks, partly in developing skills to prepare them for a field trip to the Lake District in the summer term, a study of the environment they would do there and the making of stories, books and a film. Robert felt that rural schools could become very parochial, and one way to counter that was to

> expose the children to a whole wide range of different adults, both teachers and non-teachers, with different kinds of experience and working with different groups of children, so you can have the best of both worlds. You can have the sense of community and stability, but

you can also have the kind of bells, whistles and excitement that you would get in a bigger, whizzier kind of environment.

The fact that they were vertically grouped made it

> easy for traditions to arise. It's very much now in the younger children's minds that one of the things that's part of life in this class is the link with George Ross School ... It's something for them to look ahead to, and when they do arrive there will already be two year groups who are quite experienced in this sort of thing, so that you never lose that first impetus.

There were many examples of the productivity of bringing different groups of children together, especially in personal and social development. Special needs children were paired with Bradfield children, who provided excellent coaching:

> The task is simple additions. Lily writes her name several times in different columns, and then looks at the sums, 15+3, 17+2, and 14+4. David helps, reading the numbers out, encouraging her, asking her to think again, and when right, 'Write it down then.' 'Now this is a hard one, 21 add 6.' Lily counts from 21 to 27 ... Later, David shows Lily how to use the computer. The task is to draw the man whom she had talked about in a story. But she is only interested in colours. David is very patient, but Lily is only interested in filling the screen with colour. David keeps asking her, 'Why don't you draw this?' 'Don't want to,' she says. David is very good with her, doesn't push, doesn't do it for her, wants it to come from her. Lily's teacher comes in and is very cross with her because she is not listening to David. She is taken to a 'time-out' area. David continues on his own, but the task still looks difficult for him! ... Later, they are book-making. Lily draws round the coloured paper. Her drawing is a bit wobbly, and David has to hold the paper for her. 'Lil,' he calls her, affectionately.

What impressed the researcher here was Lily's application and success in the earlier task, and David's patience and skill as a teacher. Each is learning from the other in different ways:

> The teacher reads out the stories that pairs have composed around a given structure. Valerie gives Vanessa a hug. Vanessa accepts this with a smile. Later, they have to plan, do and record a journey around the school, as part of their shared work on story making. Vanessa takes Valerie, and brings her back.

> Agnes pastes her cover. She splodges the last one on Debbie's hand, because Debbie was telling her 'that's enough!' Debbie smiles up at me in some humour. Wonderful patience these children have!

Mervyn gets much praise from Robert. 'He really did participate in that!' Mervyn is delighted.

There were many other examples of aid, patience, caring, and not a little pedagogical skill and human knowledge. The Bradfield children, as critical others here, have the advantage of not having to censure their friends – the teachers do this – nor do they have ultimate responsibility for them. This leaves them free to concentrate on friendly persuasion and assistance. The combination of forces is a powerful one. But George Ross children were critical others also for Bradfield pupils. They provided new friendships, extended their knowledge and understanding of, and feeling for, humanity, tested and challenged them in new ways, and made their own distinctive contributions to joint products. They helped to bring out the best in others. Further, the two groups of pupils within the context of the critical event (the visit to the lakes) brought out the best in the teachers. They are critical others for them also. Robert, for example, commented on the team spirit during the trip:

We had wonderful times together [i.e. the adults]. On the last evening we were still talking about things at two o'clock in the morning in a very positive way. We'd sit there swapping stories of who did this and who did that. I really do think, and this is another reason why I keep going, that the adults learn just as much as the children about all sorts of things, in terms, for example, of skills and confidence. It just underlines the fact that we're still all learning, we never stop. Let's face it, it's a fairly crummy thing to do for grown-ups who are used to their creature comforts to share a dormitory with 7 or 8 children.

In itemising his gains from the project, he mentioned the 'specific mechanics of making a film'; the 'organisational challenge of working with different groups of children on different activities', which hopefully enhanced his skills in the classroom and the school; learning a lot about the personal qualities of individual children – some 'who had question marks against them' he saw now in a much more positive light, having been through this shared experience together, and he had got to know them as 'people'; and developing his range of strategies for working with them. With one boy, for example, who had 'really quite severe behavioural problems', he was able to try out a 'couple of new things', one that we 'picked up half-way up a mountainside'.

Confidence was no less a gain for Robert than it was for the children:

We all have moments of doubt about our capabilities and competence. Having successfully completed this sort of enterprise makes you feel, 'Yes, I have got a grip on things.' You almost need to continually reassure yourself of that by setting yourself these challenges, and the kind of affirmation that comes back keeps me going till next year.

The challenges are considerable and stretch one's qualities and abilities to the utmost. 'It's no good just sitting and talking about it. You have to go through your own personal pain barrier ...' This is almost a trial by ordeal of one's own competence. But if successful, the rewards are commensurately large. There is, too, some rise in competence, he feels: 'Although I'm still learning, I do make fewer mistakes now than I did.' He had made some 'very bad mistakes' to begin with, but you really do learn 'very, very quickly'. But there had to be progression, and he was always 'injecting new ingredients into what we do'.

Robert described a 'very funny feeling' he had as he climbed on the coach that was taking them to the Lakes: that the current task was finished, he'd 'set the ball rolling', or 'pushed the first domino over', and he was beginning to think of the next project. Some of his colleagues were 'slightly appalled', he thought. But it was a transitional moment that facilitated the promotion of the interconnectedness of events within his educational career:

> Last year we went away to Exmoor. That was again quite a challenging social experience because we did it in conjunction with a tough, fairly hard-bitten, basic, big urban school. The kinds of contrasts we were seeing there between the two groups of children, and the ways they were finding out about each other, added that extra dimension.

Yet another idea was to create a link with an artist-in-residence for enhancing the school field trip. Robert and the children had been very taken with the sculptures in Grizedale Forest, and he had in mind some 'community sculpture work'. Such an activity, very 'concrete and tactile', would be excellent to work on together with George Ross children. Here again we have the continuity in the mind of the critical agent at the centre of operations. It is necessary to his sense of self-generation and self-renewal.

Robert felt that the George Ross teachers had also gained, through 'the chance to work alongside mainstream children'. He knew they had particularly enjoyed this aspect:

> ... not exactly working on their own level but working close to it with some of our children in that they felt more of a sense of partnership and co-operation, whereas on the whole when they're working with their children they're very much leading, they're setting the agenda and pace. I think they found it quite refreshing from the point of view of their own careers and their own personal development ... almost to see that there is another world outside special education ... It is easy to just focus on your day-to-day routine ... I think we have been something of a breath of fresh air to them.

Robert felt this had 'opened up' their understanding of their children and given them an improved view of what they can actually achieve, leading to 'new expectations' of them back in their own classroom. He felt 'they enjoyed being with our children because they are such good company', and 'they're interesting and entertaining and nice people to be around'.

On the trip, the special needs of the George Ross children at times became a resource. For example, the play took the 'fugitives' to a ruined castle where the 'pursuer' thought he had them trapped. But

> one of the children came up with the idea that Mary as a blind person could be their guide in the castle ... So there she was as a hermit-like figure living in the castle, able to lead them through all these underground tunnels. Because she's blind she finds her way, she knows her way, and she knows her way by touch, whereas the pursuer who goes blundering in after them just bumps into everything.

One of the helpers (a part-time classroom assistant at George Ross), who worked closely with Mary in helping her relate to that particular environment purely by sound and touch, kept a diary of the experiences Mary was having. One evening during the week she produced it, and

> we sat down together and went through it and she suddenly realised that she'd written 15 to 20 pages. It struck us with great force the enormous range and depth of what Mary was getting out of this.

It was the little 'day-to-day triumphs on a personal basis' that kept them going like 'getting Lily to the top of that mountain'. The physical demands made on the children were 'quite exceptional', and some of them 'did have physical problems', but 'they did it'. Mark, for example,

> can be quite difficult to work with. He had this terrible moaning habit about everything, no matter what. But he was in my group and he led the way [on walks]. He was in front of me. He wasn't at all negative about the experience. He wasn't saying, 'I want to stop now, I want to sit down, I want to go home.' He just wanted to get up there and we were hurtling along.

In general, 'the number one quality' that impressed Robert was 'the degree of concentration that they were able to put into an individual task'. They might have 'gone to pieces' in this totally different environment, but he 'was impressed with the degree they were able to stay on task, be it something very basic like collecting different coloured rocks, or counting the tractors we could see working in the valley below'.

For Bradfield children, Robert thought the trip would be most useful to them, particularly the work with the George Ross children, in 10, 15 or 20 years' time, when they were adults. It was an 'experience for ever'. Otherwise, there had been growth in self-confidence. Parents remarked that their children seemed 'much more grown-up somehow' and 'had learnt to do x, y or z' (for example, cleaning teeth without having to be nagged). A residential trip is 'an important step in the whole process of growing up – going away from home, having to be independent, self-reliant, live with a group of your peers'. They had to develop new skills in handling expensive equipment. Then there was a range of knowledge and skills they learned, for example about how the Lake District was formed, sketching and measuring – with 'more enthusiasm to get it right in this new environment' – and writing poetry. Some had shown astonishing skills and aptitudes, for example Nicola, who took the main part in the play, was 'stunning', 'totally amazing'. In reinterpreting the experience after the event, they came up with good ideas, for example 'making a picture of the side of the old farmhouse with little individual clay bricks which they've cut out and are using to mimic this pattern of random rubble (though, sometimes, they did miss the point of something)'.

Robert was aware that this was not a well-researched record packed with evidence – all the detail was in the preparation. But he

> still can't see a lot of profit in us finding other ways to assess and record what the children have carried away from this week ... Like the monument to Christopher Wren, 'if you want to see my achievements, look around you' ... It's a very ephemeral thing, a fleeting moment.

He quite liked the feeling of things being ephemeral, because 'it keeps you looking forward, wanting to achieve new things, whereas if you see your results in the form of concrete marks and assessments and tick lists, it's almost as if things are being cast in bronze for ever and you don't move on'. It's the actual process that's important rather than any specified objectives. Also important was the effect it had on their disposition to learning:

> For all of the children the feelings that they have about the experience are so positive that it's really acting as a little engine now, driving them through this and making them want to get it right. They're still asking questions about it.

Social development was particularly strong. All in the group were of equal status with regard to the planned activities. Robert said, 'The idea was that nobody has all the answers, nor expected to have the answers. We're expected to at least find a way to look towards those answers as a team.'

There were strong ties within the group. Robert thought they looked good as a group in the film, but they did have to 'work as a group and move as a unit'. The able-bodied would help the lesser; there was no thought of leaving someone behind. Robert pointed to 'the kind of caring that was going on' in the group context. He was also pleased to see 'a significant new dimension', that is 'a lot more touching'. He felt children were wary these days of 'touching each other in a supportive and affectionate way', but because of their play and their characters they put in 'lots of hugs and lots of helping hands. It was wonderful to see them.' This was one of the ways in which the children developed means of communication among the group. There were others, some difficult to specify. The George Ross teacher, for example, made a video on the trip and

> there were some wonderful bits which he snatched where one of my children and a George Ross child are sat there and they're totally absorbed in conversation, and you think, 'Well, what are they actually talking about?' because some of Jim's children have got very, very limited vocabularies ... It was very strange that in their own way there was something going on, but no-one's really quite sure what.

They got to know more about each other. Robert said that

> we always underestimate what children can do. Living through an experience like that [i.e. the Lakes trip] just underlines the way that children have so much, and can contribute so much to an activity of this kind. It makes you step back and be a little bit humble about the whole process, and [think] maybe being an adult isn't all that special after all.

There is no more intensive way to learn about children than going on a trip – 'part of the rationale for the whole business'; 'I really do feel that I know my children very, very well indeed having lived with them for a week'. There were also high standards of social behaviour, mutual regard and support. Many of the George Ross children show signs of seriously disturbed behaviour from time to time, but in the hostel

> they were living a home life together with 36-odd other children and a large number of adults, and they really kept themselves on the spot, under control, and joined in and took their turn at sweeping ... They were actually living a social life, and we all felt that was a great achievement ... no soiled beds, no tantrums, and huge gains socially.

Personal achievement was also of a high order. In some instances, there was a 'coming-out' of individuals. The event stretched and tested them, and all rose to the occasion. There was a large amount of creative activity. Robert felt one of the major aims was to develop the 'ability to improvise, to work within a certain situation and a certain set of constraints and still deliver a good result'. They would be 'there with a particular problem, and we'd talk it through, and someone would come up with a bright idea. Most of the time it would be one of the children saying, "Look, why don't we do it this way?"' The story itself that they acted out was theirs, with Robert acting in 'a kind of editorial capacity with the aid of the children'.

These are all aspects of 'criticality'. There is a sense of certain ultimates, or at least significant advances. There are discoveries of self and 'other', new awarenesses, new skills and knowledge. These are of a different quality than those that pertain in different circumstances, such as the family, or school, where routine and structure are more prevalent. The anti-social behaviour of some children, and the lack of understanding of them by others, is a product of social circumstance, which can be alleviated by varied experiences, perhaps at the margins of mainstream work. Teachers, also, in school are constrained by numbers of pupils, time, space, resources, expectations, curriculum and teacher culture (Hargreaves 1988). These strictures are loosened, even reversed, in such events. In this case creative opportunities have been heightened by, first, bringing together the contrasting group of children; second, removing them for a week to a distant, idyllic location; and third, gearing the association into an innovative project with clearly defined, celebratory ends.

Case Study 2: Learning through friendship

The focus in this project was on an exchange between two classes of 7-year-old pupils, one from a small, all-white, rural village school, that we shall call Garfield, the other an urban school we shall call Albert Road which had some 200 pupils, 56 per cent of whom were ethnic minority children, mainly Hindu. The teachers were keen to explore whether the differences between the two schools could be used to mutual educational advantage across the whole range of the curriculum, though the promotion of racial harmony figured large amongst the aims. There was a considerable amount of preparatory work, including the establishment of relationships between the two groups concerned, involving the exchange of letters between the children. This predicated the activity on the affective relationships established between the two sets of children and the two sets of teachers. They then spent a day at each other's school.

The Garfield children visited first, travelling by minibus with two teachers. The main events of the day were (apart from meeting their friends) 1. a visit to the nearby Hindu temple, which was introduced to them by the head teacher of Albert Road, and for which they had worksheets. These worksheets had been devised by the teachers as part of a larger project to raise awareness of the Hindu religion among junior schools generally, using the temple as a resource; 2. 'playing on the apparatus' in the afternoon (they had none of this at Garfield); and 3. meeting and playing with their friends. A fortnight later, Albert Road children returned the visit with two teachers and two parents, travelling by public transport. The outstanding features of this day were the bus ride, a walk round the village and over the fields, a visit to the church (where they were welcomed by the vicar; there were worksheets for this also), and meeting, with increased excitement, and talking to and playing with, their now-established friends. The visits were the high point of the project, but there was much activity inspired by them before, in between, and after.

What, then, was the educational value of the exchange? How did it help to promote creative learning? What follows is based on observations made on the two days of the visits, of the work produced in association with them, and on talks with the pupils and teachers involved.

English

The main need, especially for Albert Road's children, was seen to be language development, and particularly enrichment of vocabulary. For many of these pupils, English is a second language, often not spoken at home. Everyday phrases outside schools are in the mother tongue. Thus, while they had picked up 'the language of the playground and the basics, they lacked the vocabulary necessary to express themselves'. The Albert Road class teacher, Jane Esmond, estimated that the project had enabled her to introduce over 300 new words. More important than the number of new words, however, was the meaningful context in which they were used, which had beneficial results for pupils' general understanding. Farooq, for example, had 'virtually no English language' beforehand, 'though he could understand what the teacher was on about'. His class teacher described him as 'like a boy behind a wall, peering over. His eyes are gleaming with what he is going to do, but he can't say anything. He is totally frustrated.' The trip to Garfield was the breakthrough. 'On the bus going over he wanted to know every two minutes when they were getting off and would his friend be there. Would he recognise his friend? And for him to actually come out and say those things is almost incredible. The speech has come, and the written work has come, beautifully presented, and a fair command of English, for him.' If Farooq was the outstanding example, they all gained, even Ifzal, who was the only one not to go. He had never been on a bus, and had been desperate to discuss their experiences with the other children.

There was detailed planning of the vocabulary beforehand. For example, Garfield have a part-time teacher who lived in Bombay as a child, and who took saris and other Indian clothes in, and told them what different parts of the dress were called – and then they dressed up in them. Though some of the boys told the researcher wryly 'we made right fools of ourselves', they were well prepared for seeing them in context and better able to appreciate other aspects of the cultures of northern India. At Albert Road also, there had been lengthy planning particularly on words they would actually use, even to phrases like 'a half return fare to Mill Road', simple vocabulary like 'path', 'pavement', 'road' and 'street', specialised vocabulary that would be used in the temple and the church, and all the little idiomatic phrases that go between. Prior formal knowledge of the words aided identification and expression on the day, and facilitated discussion and reading afterwards. For the Garfield children, one of the main outcomes was learning skills of discussion. Their teacher said, 'They've done some discussion, which for children this age is quite hard. They can talk but they can't discuss. Now when they were talking about reactions, there was a bit of "why do you think they reacted like that? Why do you think Cherry jumped around screaming when she saw the chicken? Why do you think they were so surprised to see sheep and geese?" So they were looking behind behaviour and doing some analysis.'

The project also provided considerable motivation in writing. Notable here were the letters exchanged between pupils before and after visits. They 'actually learned how to write a letter in a much more enjoyable fashion than writing a practice letter'. They were writing to real people for a real purpose, and, more than that, the letter was going to a friend, somebody they cared about, and who would write back to them. They were consequently more worried about errors, about getting it right, about 'doing their best'. They learned about spacing and layout, capital letters and full stops. And, as John noted in one letter to his friend, they used their 'best writing'.

The first letter typically referred to their own looks, background, families and interests, with expressions of anticipation and friendship, and was illustrated artistically.

I know I will enjoy the day with you, Dipak. The Hindu Temple is exciting and I like your name, I am looking forward to the apparatus.

I am nearly eight. I have brown hair and blue eyes.

We have a farm at Garfield which has sheep in. You can stroke No. 17. My hobbies are swimming, catching butterflies, collecting money and stickers. I have one dog his name is pip his birthday is on may 22nd. Please write back soon. Good bye for now.

Letters were also exchanged afterwards. They did not only write to friends. They also sent 'thank you' letters to teachers. Even Farooq, who found writing very difficult, managed one of these:

Dear Mr Harrison and Miss Andrews, We like your school garden and we need your garden because it is nice and we have not got a garden. We need a tree please. Thank you very much for letting us come.

From Farooq

There were follow-up letters in the last week of term. Sheila and Gita had struck up a good friendship and were developing this and their learning from each other.

Dear Gita

I hope you have a nice birthday did you get your birthday card? I am looking forward to the summer holiday because you will be coming to my house. I would like to know what you eat in English

I like your mum very much.

Some, it must be said, were not so hopeful ('this shall most probably be the last time I'll talk to you so good bye'), but others wanted telephone numbers, urged replies, and conveyed expressions of genuine friendship. A Garfield child, for example, had palled up with Farooq. He found writing very difficult, but he made a big effort to get his point across on this occasion: 'I like you a lot Farooq I want you to come again with the school please come again we went to the Hindu Temple.' There were other written pieces. Some of the Garfield children, for example, composed poems about their experiences. This seemed the most appropriate medium for some of the sentiments roused on the day of the Albert Road children's visit:

> Waiting at the bus stop
> Waiting for the bus
> Clapping and cheering
> Waving and Smiling
> Bus comes along some on bus
> but they don't make a fuss
> We have a good day
> Until the end
> but first we go to the Church we see the graves and say a prayer
> Then to go home
> Waiting at the bus stop again
> Nearly missed it nearly missed it
> but this time we don't make a fuss.

And of the day of their own visit to Albert Road, one wrote this:

> We all went to Albert Road It was very fun
> We went on the Apparatus And then it just begun
> Swinging running climbing Jumping riding balancing rolling bumping
> and some of us was falling off some of us were diving high doing somersaults in the sky but time went rolling by
> leave the hall
> and go back to Garfield school.

The children found new pleasure in their *own* areas. Garfield children described their visit to their own church (a new experience for most of them!), referring in quite rich vocabulary to things they had found interesting like 'the creepy scary stairs', 'the key to the door which was as big as my hand', 'the dead mouse and two live toads in the graveyard', 'the bread table', 'the stained glass window with colours of red, purple, blue, yellow, pink and green', 'the old pump for the organ', 'the weather vane and lightning conductor'.

Albert Road children also wrote accounts, some, like John, feeling inspired to poetry:

Garfield Church
I like going to the church
Because I go to church
The church is big with three altars
And the big pulpit
And the place where the choir sings
And the big bibles
The rector opened his organ and
Miss Andrews played the organ
She played it very well
We went up the tower
It had a few steps
The tower was small
There was a font where baby gets christened
I enjoyed going there.

Mathematics

If language both spoken and written was seen as the area of study which stood to benefit most, this was because of its central importance to the rest of the curriculum. It is in some ways inappropriate to itemise contributions made to other curriculum areas, for a distinctive aspect of the exchange was the way in which it promoted a sense of holistic, integrated, experiential, pupil-centred curriculum. As one of the teachers remarked, 'The whole is more than the sum of the parts.' However, it is convenient to look at some of these areas, while bearing in mind that they are part of a 'greater whole'.

There was a certain amount of arithmetic involved, subsumed within the activity. The Albert Road children, for example, did not know how to buy a bus ticket, or how to count out the money. They did not recognise the coins even though they made frequent use of 'pretend' coins in the classroom. They knew they had to get it right on the bus, and that made the difference. They also had to study the clock and consider distances, and 'how long it would take'. They had to make out a route to Garfield and mark it on a map in their folders. On the map were questions asking them to calculate certain distances between key points in the vicinity. They also made a sundial, inspired by one they had seen at Garfield Church, one their teacher had brought in, and one they had seen in a book. 'Normally this was quite a difficult thing to introduce', but because they had seen one at Garfield, it meant something concrete. This went into the playground when the sun came out, and the children were seen actually measuring the time sections and the shadow.

Environmental studies

The whole project might easily be described as an exercise in 'environmental studies' as anything else. The town children, particularly those from ethnic minorities, lacked experience of the countryside. The village children had not been in a town, especially the kind of urban area of the type where their friends were situated. The most notable feature of the trip to Garfield for Albert Road children was the 'school garden', and they were very impressed that the houses 'all had big gardens round them', and were all 'different'. They were very appreciative of the countryside, the sheep, the chickens, the geese, the trees. As we have seen, there were pleas for 'gardens' and 'trees' in their own playground. On the walk around Garfield, the children had pointed out to them, among other things, a thatched roof, a combine harvester, 'The Old Bakehouse', a burglar alarm, a notice reading 'A school for poor children', and Garfield House. At the bottom of the village they climbed over a stile and walked across the fields, rehearsing here and there the country code, and admiring the sheep and chickens. The Garfield teacher, Susan Andrews, was keen to show her pupils a contrast to their own area, and to cultivate skills of observation. She teaches them to look and learn from their immediate environment and surrounding areas so that when they reach their secondary school they will have the necessary skills to cope with more academic work in history and geography. What did Albert Road children observe? One noticed the quietness: 'We walk round Garfield/It is so quiet you can hear with ease a sound …' Kaushik 'liked the little village and the houses'. And the thrill, novelty and educational experience of the bus ride is evident from his account: 'I liked the bus. I sat on the top and I looked out the window and I saw trees and when you go on buses you look as if you are going to crash.' Another child who sat on the top floor of the bus saw 'a flat house with straws and there was a net on the house, then we saw a boy sitting on a gate'.

Physical education

Undoubtedly the greatest attraction at Albert Road for Garfield children was the apparatus. They have none at their school, and they had been told about the frames, ropes, boxes, horses, benches, bars and mats that filled the hall at Albert Road. So deprived were some of the Garfield children in this respect that one child asked her teacher, 'What is "apparatus"?' They had 'a few balls, a few hoops and a few skipping ropes' which they could only use 'if it was fine'. Consequently 'their co-ordination was dreadful'. If they went to Albert Road for just half-an-hour on the apparatus, that would be well worth it, according to their teacher, because her children 'don't get any PE'. Her juniors are going up to secondary schools not knowing what a rope is. One Garfield child wrote:

Going on the apparatus was a lot of fun largely because we have none.
Climbing up the rope and sliding down burning your hand but at least you get down.
Climbing up metal going to the top,
looking through classroom windows,
Watching them work and stop
Walking across the beam and trying not to fall
When you look around you soon fall off
Going on the apparatus was a lot of fun
Shame you could not come along

Nor was the visit to Garfield without benefit to Albert Road children in this respect, for Garfield School's great asset was the walled, grassed garden, with a large tree in the middle. As we have seen, this figured large in their memories of the day, as did the games and activities it facilitated. Here Cherry 'learnt to do cartwheels'.

Religious education

This was an important area, especially in view of the 'racial harmony' aim of the visits. The exchange proved a sound basis for a comparative study in religion at the children's own level of thinking. They were encouraged (through brief introductory talks, worksheets, informal guidance, and considerable freedom) to explore the special features of these places of worship, to discuss them among themselves, and in doing so to reach out towards an understanding of a culture which in certain respects was markedly different from their own.

In the temple, the children were particularly impressed by 'God's Bell', the removal of shoes, the gods, the colourful and intricate decorations, the swastik, the food offerings. They had the advantage of some prior work and some worksheets to guide them round. The teachers themselves were provided with notes on the temple's chief features and history. The children later wrote:

Ting ting the bell – ring it ring it hear it go – Let's go in – But wait we can't get in we have to take our shoes off. But why. Well because they are made of cow's skin. Yes and they are not allowed to touch or eat meat that's why.

Going to the temple was a lot of fun ... we went into a room where they played some of their own sports which had rather funny names.

They had statues called Ganesh the God of wiseness and good friends, Shiv, Durga the Mother of the Universe ... All these statues are very bright and colourful ... there were seven bhavans, the Gods' houses. It was very enjoyable in the Temple area.

I like the colour in the Temple with shapes and God Fruit and oranges sweets and apples. They are juicy and they give Indian food in plates. The god was dressed in wonderful colours with necklaces and rings.

I liked the horses on the wall, and the bell.

I like doing the work sheets Miss Andrews gave us especially I enjoyed going to the Temple and seeing all the Hindu gods. The bells were loud but they were like god's doorbells.

Susan Andrews (the Garfield teacher) confirmed that they had enjoyed the temple, 'particularly the artistic children. They really did enjoy the colour.' In their classroom they had pictures, photographs, prints of the temple and Indian garments on the walls. They were able to explain what they were: 'Swastiks, Hanuman, Ganesh, Vishnu, Sari, Choti, Chemise, Scarf, Skirt.' They had remembered them well from a fortnight before.

An unexpected occurrence at Garfield Church heightened the significance of the visit for the few Muslim children from Albert Road. Scratched on the end of one of the pews Shakeel and Farooq found the Muslim star and crescent. No one knew why they were there. That 'brought such a lot of delight and pleasure to them, and they linked straight away ... That sparked off quite a lot of work when we actually came back.' There was 'a lot of comparative work' afterwards. The phrase 'Holy Book' became commonplace in the Albert Road classroom.

For the Garfield children, the RE project for the term was about 'the family and the rules we abide by, and the bigger family of the world, and looking at the people from different cultures'. The teacher 'carried that on and introduced them to the idea of children who had different colours from them, had different foods, spoke different languages and what *they'd* feel like if they were suddenly thrust into a school where the children spoke a totally different language from them. And they all talked about it, and said it didn't matter what colour people were. It was what the person was like that matters. And really it was quite new to all of them, this idea of mixing with other children.'

The sense of common cause was heightened by the discovery that the temple had certain things in common with church. There was a 'holy book', 'gods', interesting stories, prayers, singing, bells for organ or piano, the same kind of moral messages as, for example, symbolised by the swastik, and the fact that much of the information in the temple was in English as well as Gujarati, increasing the sense of 'openness'. This was increased yet more by the welcome and hospitality afforded the visitors.

At times, some of these activities (sampling other cultures, visiting temples, etc.) have elsewhere been criticised as mere tokenism, compounding the racist nature of society rather than tackling it. The references above to the Garfield children's appreciation of the artistic merits of the temple might be interpreted by some in this light. But there are a number of answers to this. First, the artistic features are an important component of the Hindu religion (as of many others). As Haigh (1987) has argued, 'there are many points at which the boundary between arts education and RE become blurred, just as worship and artistic expression often seem part of the same whole' (p. 19). Second, in any event, the children's interest represented the integrated nature of the whole activity. Third, even if the Garfield children had visited the temple on their own, and done nothing else, it might be regarded as a very useful introduction to the Hindu religion and culture, given their almost total lack of prior knowledge (one would, however, look for it to be followed up, and developed). Fourth, the activity was not decontextualised, but grounded in the affective relations of the multi-ethnic group of children. Finally, it is clear that these young children had grasped some of the basic comparative religious elements (gods, a holy book, the use and meaning of signs and stories, the 'binding' nature of religion). Their ability to do this also supports those who argue against an invariant developmentalism in children's cognitive abilities, and for their readiness to entertain abstract concepts and some quite difficult principles (see Lee and Lee 1987; Pollard 1987; Short and Carrington 1987).

Social and personal development

'Mixing' was arguably the greatest achievement of the project. This was certainly so for the Garfield teacher, for her children 'find mixing difficult', having had few opportunities to broaden their experiences in meeting other children, let alone those of a different ethnic group. They were also unused to mingling with much larger numbers of people, as they would have to do some day when they went to secondary school. At Garfield, there were only eighteen juniors. When they arrived at Albert Road, there were another twenty-two to play with, and at lunchtime nearly 200: 'And they did play with them all, I mean, none of them sat around looking lost.' The fact that many of these children were to go to the same secondary school was another gain, establishing links across what can often be a difficult transition (Measor and Woods 1984). From the very first, these two groups of children developed a strong sense of friendship. Individual links were forged through the letters, which received added sparkle through the work being done on the planning for the exchange. These friendships, therefore, mattered within the context of their lives, and of the total framework of the curriculum. And some of the excitement of the special events arranged was shared with these associations.

These individual friendships gained also from being involved in the meeting of two larger groups, indeed two communities. The fact that these pleasures were being shared with others dispelled shyness and reservation, heightened anticipation and excitement, and helped to promote a sense of inter-regional and inter-ethnic community. This in turn reacted back on relationships within their own group, for 'it broke down a lot of barriers within the classroom, the little cliques that had formed the little groupings'. There were three processes in train, therefore: the personal bond of one-to-one friendships, the culture and identity of the group as a whole as the two classes came together, and developments within individuals.

The latter can be illustrated by one or two of the more astonishing examples, for example Darren. At Albert Road, the Garfield children had planned to stand in the doorway and say their names. His teacher thought, 'Darren will never manage this, he will die. You know, stand in a doorway with twenty children looking at him, because he's no self-confidence at all. But no! "I'm Darren," he said, and he walked in. Now for him to walk across that room with all those eyes looking at him was marvellous, because I really didn't think that he could cope.' Even Carl, who 'can't mix, and doesn't know how to play, stood and talked to them. He didn't actually stand on the outside and do nothing.'

One girl, aged seven, who was the only girl in that particular age group at Garfield, may have given the impression of being backward, 'not very academic, struggling, and can't read. And she had a whale of a time the day they came over here because she'd got all these little friends, and she is a friendly little girl. I've never seen her so happy in the playground among her own kind, she came out of her shell, had a field day.' The researcher's own memory of her is watching her skip around the playground with two of her friends from Albert Road.

They were worried about one boy from Garfield who on one occasion had asked a teacher 'Are you a Paki?' They worried about what he might say to a child, if he could say such a thing to a teacher. His friend was Larry, an Afro-Caribbean, and they were very wary of each other at first. But in fact when they got back from Albert Road it was that child who said, 'Can I write to Larry?' Larry himself could at times be 'a most difficult child, and yet when he went over there he was super ... he's remembered everything. He's a child who doesn't mix much but he thinks a lot and there's an awful lot of work come from him.'

The extent and nature of friendships was evident from letters, conversations, behaviour. The arrival of the bus from Albert Road was a high point. Friendships proffered in the letters, consolidated on the trip to Albert Road, now blossomed, free of reserve and constraint, and secure in the knowledge that feelings were reciprocated: 'When we went to the bus stop I was very excited. I couldn't wait to see my friend.' The Garfield children were equally excited. As they waited, Darren remembers, 'I was excited. We went to the bus stop waiting for a bus; "you'd better hurry up it's half past 10 in the morning".' And Avril expressively described this scene in verse:

> Waiting at the bus stop
> Waiting for the bus
> Never seems to come
> Suddenly pop up
> Shy and happy faces ...

At the end of the day: 'Gosh! the bus is already there, Miss Andrews is running to catch the bus. She caught it and we wave our sad goodbyes.' Privileges were freely offered: 'We have a game called chuckle egg and I will bring it to school when you come. You will be allowed to have a go on chuckle egg.' Hopes *and* fears were expressed:

> I will be looking forward to seeing you ... do come soon or I might forget what you look like and I collect the same things as you ... I have got 1,000 key rings; I had 20 pound once and I bought all key rings with it but my mum wasn't too pleased and you can imagine that.

Promises were made: 'I am drawing you a big Donald Duck.' Presents were exchanged: 'My friend gave me a bracelet.'

Sheila and Gita were perhaps the best example of 'hitting it off', which they had done immediately on meeting at Albert Road. The Garfield children had had 'such a marvellous time, they didn't want to come home. Sheila got out of the minibus looking so miserable and her mother said that she talked from the moment she got in non-stop the whole evening, about the temple, the apparatus, her friends, the children she'd met and how marvellous it was.'

Sheila and Gita exchanged gifts at Garfield, held hands and arms, gave each other piggy backs, and talked incessantly. They phoned each other between visits, arranged for other, independent meetings in a truly blossoming relationship which spread to their families. Gita's mother accompanied them on the trip to Garfield. 'Sheila's Mum said that she would like to go to the temple', and they were trying to arrange it. The effects thus spread at certain points into another generation.

Cultural integration was all part of the mixing. There were no apparent barriers. The Garfield children took a delight in their friends' names, expressed with genuine pleasure: 'I know I will enjoy the day with you, Dipak. The Hindu Temple is exciting and I like your name.' The Albert Road children who spoke English as a second language signed their names in English and in their mother tongue. Some taught their friends at Garfield how to write *their* names in their first language. Amina actually sent a song in Bengali 'to the children of Garfield school', though its translation would have to wait until a future visit! Their teacher reported that 'one or two of them who got given the white children got a bit sort of peeved really, especially the older children, they wanted one from a different country, please'.

This shows not only their enthusiasm, but also the extent of the Garfield children's ignorance, for most of the black children from Albert Road had been born in Britain. Such a mistake is perhaps typical of schools in the 'white shires', but it was soon to be rectified. The 'ethnic minority' friend was something special, sought by these children through a feeling of comradeship. Apart from the relationships forged, there is considerable educational potential within the children as culture-bearers. Most of these were second or third generation British, but some still have strong family connections in India, Bangladesh and Africa, whom they visit regularly. As one teacher remarked, 'As they themselves acquire more command of English they could tell others about visits to Bangladesh or India or wherever, and if they hear it first hand from a child, that is going to be far more valuable than reading it up in a boring book.' An interesting corollary to this is that Sheila could understand Gita's English far more easily than she could Gita's mother's English. In general, one clear educational function in these new relationships was evident in the amount of help the children gave each other in the worksheets. The Albert Road teacher was 'fascinated by how some who were normally reticent helped others'.

The community spirit was evident during lunch at Garfield. This was taken in the playground, as fortunately it was a sunny day, and notwithstanding the privation of sitting on hard tarmac, it became a considerable social event. The children brought picnics, and sat down with teachers and parents, and talked, ate, and shared their food. The sharing was an important expression of friendship and another aspect of 'mixing'. Gita's mother had herself brought some sweetmeats, which she handed round.

After lunch there were games, and running about in the 'garden', playing 'tig', races, and the 'A-Team', or playing with toys in the playground (one group, their bottoms up in the air, huddled around some 'space invaders'). At Albert Road, too, they had indulged in uninhibited play. The boys had been fascinated by the pond in a corner of the playground, looking for tadpoles, bounding up and down on the board, climbing up a rope. It seemed important that the days included these 'letting off steam' sessions in each other's company, and taking advantage of the other's resources, allowing time to work off energies and excitement as well as to cement relationships in the joyous hurly-burly of play. As one teacher, reflecting on an alternative programme for a future occasion, commented, 'Perhaps we could ship them off to somewhere like Roman Fields where there are some swings and just let them have a play. Just literally play together, because I mean that is a lot of it, playing with each other.' The two days of the visits were very full, exciting, demanding and exhausting. Atul sums it up in simple style: 'When we went home I was tired. I like the day. I was really tired. It was good that day.'

This exchange provided a great educational boost to these children, and to their teachers. It was a cathartic event, inducing a high level of awareness and motivation, sparking off developments across the curriculum, but in ways closely integrated within the person of the child and strongly related to the child's own concerns. It rose above the institutional level of the school, placing all the activity firmly within the context of everyday life. It made use of resources readily and cheaply available in the everyday world, and within and between the people involved. The establishment of friendships and the degree of freedom allowed for these to develop ensured that all was anchored in the children's worlds. From this basis, several reached new heights of achievement, understanding and appreciation in the work associated with the project – the development of language, writing, mathematics, religious education, physical education, environmental studies, etc. But the main achievement was the platform itself – the personal and social relationships established. New identities were forged as barriers were overcome, confidence established, abilities harnessed, so that several children were seen to do things they had never done before, that some, indeed, suspected they were incapable of doing. This was coupled with the social development involved in the forging of links across regions, across generations and especially across cultures.

Conclusion

Breakthroughs in learning challenge the status quo, make the familiar strange, review conceptions of self that may have been unduly fashioned by structures, identify ideology and rhetoric, rise above and contextualise alienative forms. They are potentially empowering through what Freire (1972) calls 'conscientizacao', which 'enrols [people] in the search for self-affirmation' (p. 20), and which makes them subjects who know and act, rather than objects who are known and acted upon (Anderson 1989, p. 260).

Breakthroughs feature strong emotion, which engages the whole person in the learning activity, rouses passion and sensitises the mind. There could be no more powerful motivation to learn, nor more intensive and extensive honing of the learning faculties. They free the learner from the grip of others' knowledge and restrictive assessments of their worth. They provide strength in new-found knowledge, newly discovered abilities and newly developed skills. They lead to self-enhancement and new appreciation of relationships with others. They provide a vantage point from which to survey other areas of learning of different types, and establish a marker to aspire to in future educational pursuits.

The question remains as to whether the cases discussed here are real breakthroughs, or whether they are isolated moments, seductive episodes that give the appearance to both teachers and pupils of empowerment, but ultimately deny the reality of it. This would be too broad a sweep of a judgement, since there would always be some gains in terms of knowledge and skills which had relevance to other areas. Ultimately, however, degree of success will depend on a context generated by a number of factors to do with leadership, collaborative cultures, and commitment to a cause, reflective practitioners, a relational idea in the curriculum and some flexibility and space for teachers. Above all, the vision must be maintained, far-sighted, but realistic. Robert, even in the darkest hour of creativity – 1994 – was 'still smiling and viewing the year ahead with our usual blend of optimism tempered by experience'. While he and others like him are still there and while there is flexibility in the system, critical students remain on the agenda. Properly identified and contextualised, breakthroughs can aid in their development but other factors such as the rise of central control over the curriculum and pedagogy have also affected this development and the next case study shows some of these constraints and how teachers in the 2000s manage to maintain breakthroughs in learning.

6 Countering learner 'instrumentalism' through creative mediation

Introduction

Educational reform in England and Wales in the late 1980s and 1990s included four specific features: the introduction of a National Curriculum, national assessment tasks (SATs), Ofsted inspections, and the prescribed literacy and numeracy hours in primary schools. The extensive PACE research found that teachers' predominant response to the reforms 'was one of incorporation, in which many teachers were able to adapt the changes into existing ways of working – at least to some extent' (Osborn *et al.* 2000, p. 68).

However, they also found that a significant group of teachers was able to respond more actively to changes through what they termed 'creative mediation' (Osborn 1996). They identified four forms of this – protective, innovative, collaborative and conspiratorial (Osborn *et al.* 2000). Research into creative teaching, carried out during the same period as the Pollard research, found that the teachers who worked creatively 'appropriated' the reforms to maintain their creative practice (Woods 1995, p. 8). Other research suggests that the reforms as a whole reduced the use of teachers' experience and their knowledge of children and created a 'hurry along' climate (Dadds 2001).

One of the dangers of an unmediated reform, a compliant response (Osborn *et al.* 2000), is that 'instrumentalism' (Pollard *et al.* 2000) becomes predominant, resulting from the pressure to 'deliver' (Dadds 1994) the curriculum to increase achievement levels. The PACE researchers concluded that where teaching responses were most conformist it was 'difficult to avoid the sense of children in flight from an experience of learning that they found unsatisfying, unmotivating and uncomfortable' (Pollard *et al.* 2000, p. 103). The authors' 'broad overview of the PACE data on pupils suggests that many were playing the system, were reserved, were bored, were risk averse and were shy of engagement in learning' (ibid., p. 290).

We see engagement in learning for primary learners as 'child meaningful', suggesting that pupils make sense of learning on their own terms, based on their interests. Learning takes place best when a mutually shared understanding between teachers and pupils is built through negotiative discussion (Woods 1995). Central to meaningful learning is a sharing by teachers of the processes of exploring knowledge and the institution of pedagogy relevant to their experiences and interests.

The 'dissatisfiers' (Herzberg 1971) of learning – those aspects that demotivate learners – may well become dominant if meaningful learning is not pursued. Where this is the case, assessment regimes can result in learners devaluing subjects even when they achieve high grading (Pollard *et al.* 2000). Learning identities are then constructed as compartmentalised 'pupil' identities based on a pragmatic approach to learning (Duffield *et al.* 2000).

We wondered how teachers who valued creative teaching were managing to maintain learner commitment and meaningful learning in the wake of more insistence on direct class-based teaching. One of our studies focused on the way four teachers have creatively mediated these developments and how learners responded. The most significant of the teachers' mediations involved the explication of teacher intentions, the reconstruction of a relevant pedagogy and the development of a language to enable learners to take part in an evaluation of teaching and learning practices.

This project was carried out on 17 days from October to December 1999 and in May 2000 with three classes of Years 5 and 6 (ages 10 and 11) bilingual, mainly Bangladeshi learners in an inner city school – Best End school. An ethnographic research approach was employed which included classroom observations, the writing of field notes, the collection of relevant school documents and recorded conversations with teachers and learners. A semi-structured conversation schedule was prepared for interviews with teachers and learners. During these conversations issues of school life were highlighted and alternative, oppositional and differing perspectives were invoked to generate debate. Photographs of classroom and school activities were used as a stimulus for conversation, discussion and argument.

The school included a specific commitment to creative practices. Projects included: a visit to a local art gallery and a 'new technology' printing operation; the observation of a school journey at an environmental activity centre; the engagement of the learners in an afternoon workshop dedicated to the physics of bridge building with ropes; a four-week improvisation singing workshop; the use of drama to enhance curriculum priorities; and art lessons focused on highlighting different perspectives. Within the more formal curriculum – literacy, maths and science – we observed teachers using video recordings of plays, books and biological systems to support teaching programmes. An active 'hands-on' approach was adopted for science, design and technology programmes, and arts and crafts techniques were used productively by learners to design their own writing books. Learner interviews of school support staff were used in developing note-taking skills and the teachers role-played literary characters, as did learners. Alternative mathematical strategies for specific computations were explored, learner preferences were encouraged and computer programs exploring scientific areas were in constant use by small groups.

The school complied with the reforms and organised its teaching by curriculum subject, in time slots, except for occasions when they adjusted the timetable to accommodate special curriculum events. These events, such as the singing workshop, did not generally have any connections with the formal National Curriculum but they contributed to a creative culture (Jeffrey 2001a) which had a bearing on the school generally. The subject boundaries in the classrooms were strong as was the pedagogic frame (Bernstein 1971), but on occasions there was a weakening of the subject classification and framing to enhance creative teaching and learning. The research period included an Ofsted inspection and observation of SATs for Year 6.

Explicating teacher intentions

One of the major developments arising from the reforms is the necessity for teachers to establish detailed objectives for each teaching period. These plans are used for the assessment of learner achievement and for accountability procedures, such as Ofsted inspections, when inspectors require evidence of progress in lessons measured against pre-determined objectives. The incorporation of these objectives was influenced by the reforms, such as an Ofsted inspection:

> I say at the beginning of a lesson 'what I want you to get out of this by the end of it'. I never used to do that. I used to assume that they would empathise with me and understand these things as if by magic. I just think that I am giving them clearer goals than I probably ever have done in my teaching career so far ... That timetable wouldn't have been there prior Ofsted, it's there and it's real, it's not Mickey Mouse. I worked it, I'm happier, the kids are happier and I genuinely think it works.
>
> (Jeffrey and Woods 1998, p. 163)

However, the Pollard *et al.* (2000) research concluded that, where the teaching was most compliant, primary learners at Years 5 and 6 had a relatively limited conception of teachers' intentions. These learners could not articulate any understanding of what they were doing and they lacked a language for talking about learning: 'A concern for the children was to find out as precisely as possible "what she wants" and to respond to well-known idiosyncrasies' (Pollard *et al.* 2000, p. 178).

Our current research found three significant factors, emanating from teacher reactions to the reforms that contributed to a clarification of teacher intentions. These were:

1   Clear teaching and learning objectives;
2   The incorporation of a significant amount of direct teaching as opposed to independent learning; and
3   The highlighting of specific technical vocabulary and concepts attached to each subject.

These were the first steps to recovering creative teaching and learning in which learners gained some control through a shared knowledge of the objectives and some space being allotted for learners to manipulate the ends (see Chapter 8). Collective engagements with the whole class encouraged a circulation of ideas in a participative approach, and the gradual ownership of the technical vocabulary made learning more meaningful. This was not discovery learning (Plowden Report 1967) but it was an attempt to bring back a form of learner control and motivation after a significant period of instrumental imperatives. To elaborate:

1   Teachers were expected to record a lesson's objectives at the beginning of each lesson, whereas previously they would have had objectives for the week or term: 'We're going to find out how poems are constructed this afternoon' (Tracy, Yr6-T). 'We're going to learn how blood flows round the body' (Carol, Yr6-T).

2   The prescriptive programmes had increased direct teaching by designating the type of pedagogy teachers employed, e.g. outline objectives and discuss knowledge to be learnt as a class, carry out a related learning activity individually or in pairs, and review and reinforce learning activity all in designated time spans over an hour. Although we have no systematic data from our current research, at least one carpet session, where all the class are gathered together, of over 45 minutes was recorded on each day we visited. Every lesson began with at least a 15-minute introduction and most concluded with a shared whole-class review of the lesson lasting at least 10 minutes. We estimated that the balance between direct teaching and independent learning in each lesson was even. Creative teaching has been shown to include direct teaching. In our earlier creativity research we found that teachers spent between 20 and 25 per cent of teaching time talking to the whole class (Woods and Jeffrey 1996). However, the nature of the dialogue has been affected by the prescriptive nature of curriculum and pedagogic programmes. The teachers in our previous research allowed time for learners to develop their own dialogues as a group, encouraged the use of their imagination and found time for 'off task' discussions (ibid., pp. 107–114). In the current research the whole-class dialogues focused more strictly on the delivery of content, such as the lesson on figures of speech in the literacy programme. Direct teaching enhanced the clarity of learning objectives:

The poem Hist Whist is read by Tracy and the children are asked to indicate what they think it is about. Then they are asked about their beliefs in the supernatural – Halloween, ghosts, going to sleep in the dark. Tracy then goes on to talk about the structure of the poem, about punctuation, stanzas, onomatopoeia, rhythm and rhyme, alliteration. The children knew about the last one. They are asked to spot other ways of writing poetry other than fiddling with the text, e.g. shape, as in the Cummings poem. One child offers metaphors – 'describe it one way and meaning another'. Tracy describes the difference between the simile and a metaphor. Personification is introduced.

(FN-9/11/99)

3 A third factor that assisted this clarification was the importance attached to technical language and concepts:

The 11 o'clock lesson was maths. The children were given a list of musical instruments with prices attached to them and Tracy talked to them for over 20 minutes about what 'range' meant in terms of a range of numbers and how they could divide up the list of prices into a set of regular 'ranges'. They then had to construct a bar graph of the ranges and find out the mode, mean and median of the set of price lists. The learning is done as a group with the teacher taking correct answers as an indication that 'we're getting there'. There were many quizzical looks as they attempted to take on new information and concepts, and language such as 'class intervals' and 'discreet data'. Tracy talks of 'interrogating' the data and 'interpreting' it. They are asked to make out some questions from the graph. 'Give me a fact,' she asks.

(FN-18/10/99)

'It was interesting because before we made the yoghurt we looked at the packaging and we learnt new words like "prototype", that I didn't know before' (Raju). The language of evaluation in this design and technology project was foregrounded by 'review, evaluation, consumer, preference, analysis, and analyse a design process'. The technical language was then re-incorporated in evaluations by learners, in some cases creatively: 'I enjoyed the Millennium Bridge workshop because when I was holding the tension of the ropes I could feel the force' (Rogina).

(Yr6)

The clear explication of objectives by teachers in our research, deriving from the reform guidelines but in a climate where the relevance of learning to pupils was maintained, lessened the ambiguity of teacher intentions.

However, as we shall show in Chapter 8, there are occasions when the teacher, though having clear objectives, might choose not to spell them out at the start of a lesson in the interests of 'discovery learning'. In these cases, the scaffolding has to be sound enough to compensate.

Reconstructing a relevant pedagogy

Knowledge in the current research was not so much 'discovered' or explored, but introduced and grappled with, to develop understanding and 'collection' (Bernstein 1971) by learners. Teachers' general objectives were concerned with achieving 'a balance of knowledge in terms of what you pass on, and what conclusions you encourage children to reach themselves. I think you can overburden them with knowledge, but you still need knowledge to provide a contact with them' (Carol, Yr6-T). However, the strategies used to make learning relevant have had to be restructured in the light of the reforms. Our earlier research showed teachers 'responding to learners' emotions, engaging interest, maintaining identity and developing learners' educational evaluations' (Jeffrey and Woods 1997, p. 17). The current research showed teachers more intent on balancing emotional reactions with learning imperatives emanating from curriculum reform and this resulted in a more pragmatic use of emotions to engage interest. A re-orientation of learner identity towards a 'pupilization' (Woods *et al.* 1999) has been a direct consequence of recent reforms but the teachers countered the more negative effects such as the differentiation of individuals by achievement grading with the development of a team identity to learning. However, they gave less priority to developing learners' educational evaluations, concentrating on engaging interest and developing a team identity.

Engaging interest

Engaging learner interest in the wake of the reforms has meant a greater emphasis on outcomes rather than process but still retaining the importance of devising strategies to encourage learners to take ownership of specific teaching and learning objectives.

> When people in my class say 'we don't like science, and we can't do maths' I feel it is a challenge. I say 'you can do maths and you will like science', and I lower their fear. That is what I enjoy about teaching, that feeling that you have won the battle to engage interest.
>
> (June, Yr5-T)

Teachers prioritised the use of media narratives, humour and role-play and the more cognitive adventure of problem posing to engage interest.

The teachers in our earlier research created atmospheres of excitement, wonder, fascination and tension to generate learners' engagement in the learning process through story telling, 'teachable moments' and developing common bonds of humanity (Woods and Jeffrey 1996). In the current research there was a greater emphasis on the use of relevant media narratives such as video representations of science and literacy narratives. The importation of video reflects the contemporary experience of children with this form of representation and the strong relationship that young people have with narrative as the main vehicle for processing experience (Fox 1989; Woods and Jeffrey 1996). The choice of a cartoon film of *Romeo and Juliet* for a Literacy Hour project was directly relevant to the learners' interest in film as a learning medium:

> 60 children sit cross-legged, hands under chins, arms crossed in laps, fingers caressing the floor in front of them, fiddling with an ear, arms crossed over hunched knees as they gaze at the television drama. One child sits with her hands resting on her knee under her chin – her body rocking gently backward and forward. Smiles and knowing looks with the eyes are expressed as a love scene is shown. They break into quiet laughter and show gentle and smiling disgust at a kiss. The thumb and finger of one boy plays with his bottom lip as he stares intently. Some fingers rest in his mouth and he grins slightly at embarrassing moments. There is some laughter and their heads and bodies begin to rock as the love scene develops. Smiles come and go. As the scene changes to a discussion between the Friar and Romeo so the giggles subside and concentration ensues. The comical parts are greeted with amusement, smiles and sparkling eyes. The pinpoint TV glare can be seen in their staring eyes. The poignant music at the discovery of Juliet's body makes them discard their smiles and they view it with straight, serious faces.
>
> (FN-27/10/99)

However, the involvement of the learners through this medium is punctuated by a focus on specific curriculum learning objectives as teachers

> interject to illuminate details of the plot and characters. Robina talks of this as being working time. Immediately it finishes Tracy asks them 'did any good come out of it?' She then asks what they thought of it but there are no answers. She asks if they thought it was sad but doesn't refer to the way the music created the atmosphere. There is then some information given about Shakespeare's language and the nature of dialect. Robina continues to supply specific vocabulary and facts and information that they should know but the young participants appeared mesmerised by the drama and appeared to reject for now the slicing up of the experience into analytical structures. Then they go back to the classroom for religious education.
>
> (FN-18/10/99)

The teachers feel the necessity to bring out the learning objectives even during a moving drama they have presented as they try to combine both creative and instrumental teaching.

Stronger 'classification and framing' (Bernstein 1971) of teaching means the use of more teacher 'performances', an affective creative teaching characteristic used sparingly in our earlier research (Woods and Jeffrey 1996). 'Tracy, the teacher, cracks a joke and the children laugh ... She is animated as she plays the Nurse from *Romeo and Juliet* with an aching back. The children laugh and turn to each other smilingly' (FN-19/11/99). The new structure of discrete lessons and the objectives-led curriculum means, for creative teachers, an increase in the construction of performances for each session to engage the learners' interest.

Creativity, in the hands of these teachers, has become part of the new reform process: 'We try and plan to be creative. It has got to be planned for. It is very rare that our teaching and learning is creative through being spontaneous. It can't be; nothing is spontaneous any more' (June, Yr5-T). In a literacy hour session, Robina and Carol did their direct teaching by acting out an extract from *Romeo and Juliet* focusing on character and differences emphasising the textual rhythms. Taking other identities such as that of a fictitious character, artist or designer is part of planning for creativity. An adventure book designed to appeal to young people is read to the learners and they compare it with a film of the book:

> The learners discuss acting a 'rage' in a film and how a character's feelings of being alone might look in a film. Trisha gets them to perform this and she also encourages one of the children to act the part of a director. The children then have to go and do their storyboard – scene setting and character behaviour or interchange.
>
> (FN-6/12/99)

Learners take the role of artists:

> Carol arranges her Yr6 class to sit around a square of tables drawing charcoal pictures of a still life scene. They smudge and shade in sections carefully and converse down their line of 'artists'. Carol again uses technical detail, for example 'warp and weft, textured, grainy'. She says they must make these come through. She makes them work in virtual silence – independently. There are fewer smiles and more concentration than other sessions. Carol asks her children, 'Can you see through the picture? What is the relationship between the objects? Can you make the softness of the cushion and a hardness of the chair more apparent?' She exhorts them to look at the 'texture, tone, composition, shape and space'. She is bringing them into the artist's world by focusing on the technology of the artist's practice.
>
> (FN-17/11/99)

The teachers also plan to

> model the kind of thought processes and questioning of the knowledge. In fact I was doing that in art this afternoon. OK, I was asking for their response, but I was responding as well, as a person not a teacher. When I am working, I am always conscious of modelling my learning. It is being able to learn about learning as well. As a teacher, I am quite conscious of wanting to be a learning model. I am not the holder of knowledge that they have to unlock.
>
> (Carol, Yr6-T)

June set up a shop in a design and technology project, with a variety of ingredients to be 'sold' to the learners so they could add them to a basic yoghurt mixture. The children decided what the ingredients should be and Joanna purchased fruit, food colourings and chocolate. Later the learners took the role of evaluators:

> 'At first it was too light so I added chocolate and it became darker and tasted better' (Opu). 'Mine tastes very nice but I do not think anyone will buy it because it doesn't look very nice' (Kibria). 'The taste and the colour were OK but it did not smell very nice. I was unsure how to change the smell' (Ishatt). 'The crinkles make it a crunchy texture' (Opu). 'I mixed and mixed and got carried away but it still tasted good' (Kibria).
>
> (FN-23/11/99-Yr5)

Young children naturally play a variety of roles (Woods *et al.* 1999) and learners' interests are engaged by opportunities to do so:

> I would give this activity 10 because at home I don't do really interesting things. It is boring at home. I love school because we do fun activities. This time I had a chance to do something on my own. When I am at home my mum is always there to help me and I don't like that.
>
> (Opu, Yr5)

By extending teacher performances into learner 'role play' teachers show how it is possible to inhabit the curriculum content and then to step outside it and examine it. The teachers were managing to teach creatively and to teach for creativity (NACCCE 1999).

Problem-posing has been a significant characteristic of creative teaching (Woods 1990, 1994, 1995; Woods and Jeffrey 1996) and has demanded mainly open-ended solutions in order to encourage learner discussion and debate about the different paths they might take. However, with more whole-class teaching, lesson limits and prescribed objectives, teachers have widened the definition of problem solving to fit the new situation by including more 'closed' problem solving. In these contexts learners face more problems which have fixed solutions like a puzzle or a quiz. Where the activity is fairly technical an appeal to the detail of the techniques can be enough to maintain a learner's interest: 'I liked learning how to put the numbers in the columns to do subtraction. If you don't do it properly you can't do the sum accurately' (Fareena, Yr6).

Offering a limited choice is an example of an approach to solving a 'closed' problem, which learners appreciate as it increases feelings of control over learning. June taught her Yr5 class two different strategies for finding the difference between two numbers – subtraction and equal addition. The learners were then invited to select one as their preference.

The teachers maintained the 'workshop' principle (Woods and Jeffrey 1996) but the same investigation is now done at the same time by all the learners. June posed a whole-class collaborative problem in a science lesson concerning

> dissolving solids. They had to predict what would happen to five contrasting solids – salt, flower, sugar, sand and Plaster of Paris – if dissolved in water. Results were analysed on the carpet as a class. 'The sand changed the water colour'; 'some did not dissolve and stayed at the bottom'.
>
> (FN-9/11/99)

This activity is another example of a relatively closed problem, an experimental problem. The search for evidence in literature is offered as another problem but treated a little more openly:

> Tracy is reading a class story of the adventures of a girl. However, they don't just have to listen; they are set a problem to solve. The author ambiguously portrays the girl as an angel. The learners have to provide some evidence for this possibility and they find phrases such as 'she floats as a cloud', 'she gets away with things', 'she smiles heavenly'.
>
> (FN-8/11/99)

The school journey provided the teachers with an opportunity to construct more open-ended problems. The Yr6 learners had to design and construct a model shelter with twigs, small branches and other natural materials. This activity completely absorbed them as they went about their task:

> Negotiations abound. 'Shall we do a square one or a triangular one?', 'Shall we add an extension?', 'Shall we have a roof?', 'Shall we use the door of your design on the structure of mine?' ... Cutting frames, supports, doors and walls to the exact size becomes both a trial and a source of satisfaction. They hold and balance the resources against one another, demonstrate muscular sawing, delve into boxes, and stand and

stare, studying the particular. They queue patiently to get their models glued together, commenting on someone else's, appropriating others' ideas whilst still discussing and arguing about the development of the shelter. Freshly glued models are carefully transported to their tables for further embellishment with eyes fixed on their creation.

(FN-7/12/99)

The learners' engagement in this creative process enhanced their awareness of learning processes: 'I liked doing the design because I liked improving it, putting on more detail'; the importance of 'choice to do it the way we wanted to'; and the opportunity to use imagination: 'I enjoyed the design because I was able to imagine myself living in it.' They articulated an awareness of the value of continual learning, 'You learn from doing things, how to do them better next time', and an awareness of experimentation: 'I liked doing the design because we could try using different things and then change them if we wanted to.' 'It is better learning by doing things because you learn by your mistakes' (FN-7/12/99).

Occasionally, where it was thought desirable and productive, the subject boundaries were weakened by the teachers to provide more problem-posing:

The children were doing a potato printing design for a cover for their school journey books. However, Carol introduced a mathematical element by insisting that they made a rotating pattern. The children were very engaged with the problem of creating and maintaining the pattern.

(FN-9/12/99)

In such ways, teachers have expanded problem-posing as a means of engaging learner interest within the parameters of increased prescriptive pedagogies that determine the pattern of every lesson and the timing of each interaction.

Developing a team identity

The current context of prescriptive programmes and SATs imperatives means that learner identities have inevitably become more reconstituted towards individual achievement in terms of standardised 'level descriptors' (QCA 1999):

'One of the teachers told us that one of us had reached level 5. I thought she was good' (Farida). 'I was happy for her but at the same time I thought I could have done better' (Lutfa). 'I once had a low mark and I was very upset. If you have the lowest mark in your class you will be very ashamed. You feel alone. Sometimes people laugh at you' (Kumol).

(Yr6)

A performativity discourse has pervaded schools (Ball 2000; Jeffrey 2002): 'Sometimes it doesn't matter so much if you don't work so hard but something important like the SATs does matter because if you do not get good marks you will have let yourself down' (Lutfa, Yr6).

The development of team identities is different from our previous research (Jeffrey and Woods 1997) in which maintaining identity was an aspect of creative teaching which specifically involved encouraging individual creative practices, strategies and discussion, debate and peer resolution of issues and learning problems (Jeffrey and Woods 1997; Woods and Jeffrey 1996). It is also different from the participative strategies encouraged in situations in which creative learning was the major approach to teaching. During the period where performativity dominates, schools developed corporate identities to respond to the market context in which their schools were compared in terms of league table results of performance. This team approach permeated the school and the classroom.

The teachers make the most of this cultural change: 'It is part of the current strategy to increase whole-class teaching so that all the children hear the answers from others and hear the information in a way that might be more acceptable to them as they share knowledge' (Tracy, Yr6-T).

The learners then take up the team culture:

> We work at the SATs to make our teachers proud of us. So that teachers can say 'you have got the highest marks of the schools in our borough'. So they can say we are the best group.
>
> (Kumol, Yr6)

However, teachers were also concerned to ensure creative learning experiences have taken advantage of team identity to encourage learner collaboration, as in the example of the school journey where the learners were asked to build a full-size shelter from material found on the edges of a wood:

> 'It was good building the shelter because we were in a team and sharing ideas' (Shereena). 'It is good to know how to work as a team, helping each other. If you forget something the other people in your team will help you. Whereas when we were doing our models each individual might only concentrate on their own and you would get less help' (Shazia). 'In our team we had to talk together and get ideas from each other. You have to know who was going to do each job. We shared the jobs out in our team' (Asheema). 'We learnt teamwork. This team was good because they gathered everything together' (Rahanna).
>
> (Yr6)

In our past research we noted workshop approaches in which groups of children carried out different investigations as part of a project and reported back to the class, so developing a contributory approach to collaboration

(Woods and Jeffrey 1996). However, in this performativity period collaboration was called teamwork, emphasising the collaborative nature of the activity as well as the knowledge gained from it. Valorising the collaborative aspect reflected a major aspect of the performativity discourse but teachers were also able to inject a participative aspect that encouraged creative learning.

Team identities bring the learners and teachers closer, in terms of school objectives, for example, in an Ofsted inspection:

> 'All the children were really sensible because they wanted to show that our school was the best school. We wanted to get a better report and we were told that if we didn't get a good report we would get into the newspaper' (Shameena). 'If we had a bad report people might not send their children to the school' (Rahanna).
>
> (Yr6)

Learners began to identify with their teachers' position in the performativity discourse:

> It is hard for the teachers to teach us such a lot and they spend a lot of time doing it. And if we don't get a 'level four story' it looks like the teachers have not worked hard enough. If we don't succeed it would have let them down because they have worked so hard trying to get us to get good marks.
>
> (Shameena, Yr6)

Other more standard strategies for maintaining personal identities, such as an appeal to cultural experience (Woods and Jeffrey 1996), were still in evidence: 'The learners prepared questions for a Buddhist visitor by firstly interviewing each other about their own religion and then collaboratively sorting out appropriate questions' (FN-18/11/99).

The new structures have led teachers to construct more whole-class 'performances' with fewer individual teacher–learner interactions but a whole-class collaborative culture has developed in pursuit of 'common knowledge' (Edwards and Mercer 1987). Focusing on commonalities, rather than differences, was a fallout of criticism of child-centred approaches to teaching and learning in the late 1980s (Alexander *et al.* 1992). Learners' identities have been reconstructed to focus more on achievement levels but these teachers have acted creatively in establishing team cultures to mitigate the negative effects of individual differentiation.

Learner evaluations

Our earlier research showed that teachers were keen to develop learner evaluations of class practices by encouraging argument and discussion of curriculum issues (Jeffrey and Woods 1997). This action created the language necessary to engage in those evaluations. Our current research showed fewer wide-ranging discussions between teachers and learners about curriculum issues and learners' individual experience and perspectives. However, we found that this did not mean that learners lacked a language to conceptualise learning and engage in evaluations.

Learning experiences were described as: intellectual organisation, 'I learnt how to make yoghurt. I have never planned things like that in my life. I learnt that I have to think about it' (Nipa); empirical experimentation, 'I thought that if you put food colouring in it would change the flavour but it didn't' (Shazia); the investigation of variables, 'I learnt that taste is not everything and that you have to think about colour, texture and how the package looks' (Farida); decision-making processes, 'I was unsure whether putting chocolate in would make it taste good or not. I learnt that you have to experiment' (Parvin) (Yr6).

The learners proposed 'fitness for purpose' solutions (Alexander *et al.* 1992) for effective learning: 'I think there should be quality noise in a classroom. When we were doing something like making the yoghurt it could be quite noisy, but when we are reading it needs to be quiet, so that we can concentrate' (Asheema). The 'doing and sitting' issue was solved with more flexibility: 'I think I would prefer to do a little bit on the carpet then have a little bit of doing and then come back to the carpet so that I remember each part easily' (Rheena) (Yr6).

The Pollard *et al.* (2000) research found that children's experience of classroom assessment was 'remarkably consistent' (p. 152). They

> are aware of assessment only as a summative activity and use criteria of neatness, correctness, quantity and effort when commenting on their own and others' work ... There is no evidence that teachers were communicating any of this formative or diagnostic assessment to their pupils.
>
> (ibid., pp. 152–153)

In our research, learners who had been made aware of teaching and learning objectives, engaged and made to feel part of a team, were able to understand some of the advantages of a formative assessment for learning:

'I like getting the marks because I like knowing where I have gone wrong so I can put it right. And then I can improve' (Parvin). 'I like doing them because we can work independently. When we go to secondary school we will have to work independently and no one will be helping us' (Kumol). 'It is good working on your own because when you do your SATs test you have to do it on your own. It is like a challenge to yourself to see how independent you can be' (Farida). 'I love it when Tracy gives me back my marks. Then I tell other people what I got and they tell me their results and we can see how good we are. If someone gets more than me then I think I should work harder and become as good as them' (Shuheema).

(Yr6)

In some circumstances low achievers became demotivated and dysfunctional. In such circumstances they intended to deny the tests, not wanting to talk about them, desiring not to be seen as 'getting it wrong' or asserting that 'tests are boring' (Pollard *et al.* 2000). Our sample of Yr6 learners included 12 per cent who were 'excused' from the SATs revision process by their teachers because they thought it would be distressing for them if they found themselves failing too often. However, the pupils themselves did not, perhaps surprisingly, perceive this as a benefit but as a denial of their rights to take part in the revision process:

> 'I wanted to do them all, especially the maths. But in some ways I didn't want to do them because they are too hard' (Farheena). 'You don't understand. We want to do them but we want to understand them so we can do them' (Rogina). 'So we can be brave and good' (Shaheeda).

(Yr6)

This could also be seen as an example of the wish to retain team membership.

Learners acted to challenge negative emotions induced by testing through self-examination and reflection: 'Sometimes when you get a low mark you know you are better than that. You know that you didn't try very hard. That happened to me once. I sort of knew I had not tried very hard so I was not that disappointed with the low mark' (Lutfa, Yr6).

Involvement in the process of assessment enabled debates to emerge about how to improve assessment procedures:

> 'They could let the teachers decide on our levels' (Raju). 'The problem is that if you are the teacher's pet, you get higher marks' (Shumeena). 'I would give extra marks for those who did it quickly but allow lots of time for all of us' (Shereena). 'The problem with that is that it might encourage some of us to rush it' (Parvin).

(Yr6)

They recommended that assessment policy and procedures include: the introduction of graded tests, 'Those people who didn't do well in the first test should be able to have another one that was easier for them' (Raju); streaming, 'I would have groups doing tests that are similar. Those that can do the hard tests would do them together and those that could only do the easier ones would do them together' (Raju); adjusting the test instrument, 'I would have tests with answers in, where they give you a clue' (Wahidua);

less testing and more effective collaborative assessment for learning, 'You could put everyone's ideas together and choose an answer. That would help everyone as well; it would help them to understand' (Shumeena) (Yr6).

Evaluations of the assessment process itself broadened to include evaluations of the relationship between testing and valued learning experiences. The learners reflected on the process of curriculum and assessment and articulated some general observations: 'I would prefer to do a project for a week or some maths for a week and then have a test. You would do better this way because you knew the work' (Shereena, Yr6). A concept of balance was invoked: 'I like tests and doing things because tests get your brain to work but it is also nice to do things like make slippers. It is fun and you get to relax, but I like my brain working too' (Mehedi, Yr6). The balance between direct teaching and learning and active learning was also debated and provided evidence of their awareness of learning processes:

> 'It is better learning by doing things because you learn by your mistakes and you can improve things. It is better than sitting on the carpet and listening to someone' (Asheema). 'You use more of your own ideas when you're doing things' (Shameena). 'However, you can generate ideas and ask questions on the carpet' (Farida).
>
> (Yr6)

In spite of a decrease in open classroom discussions about curriculum and learning, pupils had developed a language to conceptualise learning and pedagogy, due to the development of a team culture. Two of the factors that influenced these competencies were: making teaching intentions manifest and developing learner relevant pedagogies.

Conclusion

Croll (1996, p. 156) argues that schools are 'embedded in a dynamic network of personal identity, values and understandings that are constantly developing in the light of internal and external interaction, pressure and constraint'. Our current research shows how teachers have built on the more public expression of educational purposes and processes to make their intentions clearer and to a limited extent involving learners in greater knowledge of the teaching and learning process. Second, the reconstruction of a relevant pedagogy as a creative mediation by teachers assists the maintenance of a dynamic interaction between learners and learning. One of the consequences of the combination of these two approaches has been to generate a language for learners to articulate their awareness and understanding of teaching and learning. However, in order to fully challenge 'instrumentality', learner voice and negotiative discussion (Woods 1995) needs to be more fully incorporated into the curriculum organisation and pedagogy. Although our research found learners to be aware and articulate we did not find much evidence of teachers incorporating learners' perspectives in an evaluation of their teaching and learning practices.

The argument for taking account of learner perspectives in colleges, schools and classrooms has a broad base. It is a human rights issue enshrined in the United Nations Charter, article 12, a citizenship and democracy issue (Davies 1999; Young 1999), an accountability device (Ofsted 2001), a market-consumer issue (Ball 1997), a vehicle for improving schools (Rudduck *et al*. 1996), a strategy for increasing learner commitment and motivation (Rudduck and Flutter 2000), and an opportunity to enhance learner collaboration with teachers (Donnington *et al*. 2000). The incorporation of learner perspectives into educational programmes enhances commitment to school programmes (Rudduck and Flutter 2000) and can assist new goals such as lifelong learning (Claxton 1999).

Looking to the future the general conclusions of the Pollard *et al*. research were that

> the real challenge is not whether we can improve on each and every measurement of performance in the basics but how we can create policies and practices that enable a virtuous circle to develop between standards, imagination, capability, flexibility and self confidence. We must combine knowledge, skill, creativity and commitment to learning.
>
> (Pollard *et al*. 2000, p. 316)

The virtuous circle needs to include the incorporation of perspectives to establish a common platform for engagement with teaching and learning. The outcomes would be more effective teaching and learning, more commitment from learners and a closer relationship between teachers and learners. In these times of more central control a range of strategies is necessary to maintain this platform and the next chapter provides another case study of how two schools took advantage of a new 'discourse of creativity' supported by government to recover creative teaching and learning experiences.

7 Recovering creative teaching and learning

Using critical events

The predominant response during the 1990s to the reforms in primary schools 'was one of *incorporation*, in which many teachers were able to adapt the changes into existing ways of working – at least to some extent' (Osborn *et al.* 2000, p. 68 – original emphasis). There were a few isolated examples of appropriation (Woods 1995; Jeffrey and Woods 2003) or creative mediation (Osborn *et al.* 2000) in which teachers managed to preserve what they thought best about their practice and protected children, to some degree, from what they considered to be the worst effects of the change. As we saw in the last chapter, in the early 2000s some primary schools attempted to manipulate the heavily prescribed curriculum and pedagogy to ensure some creative teaching and at the same time others created spaces for it, legitimising their actions by invoking some of the policy statements that employed the creativity discourse. These situations have been seized upon by teachers and schools recently to first confront constraint and then begin to re-establish creativity teaching and learning through the reintroduction of a series of 'critical events'. This is the focus of this chapter in which two schools used the critical other (Woods 1995; and see Chapter 5) to lever open opportunities for creativity teaching and learning.

With the testing of teachers' pedagogies against the National Curriculum, the organisation of the curriculum in primary schools became subject-centred once again, as it had been prior to the 1960s – although some schools had continued the practice throughout this period. Teaching and learning in the new millennium in primary schools was now wholly organised around a strict timetable. 'Everything was being squeezed. We found that a lot of the music, dance, PE and the artistic things were being put on the back burner' (Veronica, Head-S). There was a fragmentation of learning time into smaller and smaller slots of either 40 minutes or an hour and ten minutes (Jeffrey 2002, 2003):

> The topic approach completely and utterly went in the Juniors. The children were losing the skills of being able to apply different concepts to different situations and we really felt that the topic work of the past was extremely good because children were able to link lots of different

things together to see an overall picture. We lost that for some time because each subject became timetabled.

(Veronica, T-S)

The opportunity for individualised attention had diminished:

> In a regimented, tight curriculum you don't have the chance to see a different side to the children. We're too prescriptive in our teaching and we have to follow the curriculum and we have to do this and that, whereas in the olden days something might happen in the day and you could go off and have a wonderful learning day but not necessarily following set rules and plans and by the children taking the lead you get so much more out of it.

(Tracy, T-S)

Even in those schools that have appropriated the new initiatives and are famous for their creative approach, a full timetable may operate in which learners go to subject teachers for their age and level of ability for four days of the week (Jeffrey 2003). The schools in this study made use of the critical event to challenge this development and revise and redress past practices.

The critical event

The structure of a critical event, as exemplified by Woods (1993), goes through well-defined stages of conceptualisation, preparation and planning, divergence, convergence, consolidation and celebration. The events he identified stirred up the adrenalin, sharpened senses of awareness, marshalled energies and abilities, even summoning up new ones. The experiences were cathartic, providing a spark which touched off individuals and groups and which led to revelations about oneself and others. People realised that they could both enhance the group and be enhanced by it, that their own worth was valued and that they could value the work of others. There was respect and dignity for both self and others (Woods 1993). Some of the schools we studied at the end of the 1980s and during the early 1990s feared the critical event was doomed under the new legislation (Woods 1993, 1995; Woods and Jeffrey 1996; Jeffrey and Woods 1998).

The schools we focus on here – Suburbia and Tunnel – were still subject to the dominant discourse of performativity. They still had to comply with the imperatives of Ofsted inspections. The teachers regularly tested their children in Years 2–6 in spite of government requirements only to do it for Years 2 and 6. (All the data in this chapter are from teachers or other adults as specified.) They used a subject-centred timetable and used pre-packed curriculum programmes that conformed to the National Curriculum and they laid out the year's programme of study for all to see:

There's always that worry that if somebody came in and said, what you have done this term, you still worry about justifying it. There is that worry that somebody might not like it, there's always that worry that someone might come in and look at your books. It's people watching, it's a bit like 'Big Brother' really. They're not there all the time but they're in the back of your head like scars.

(Marilyn, T-S)

However, the schools employed two specific strategies to prime creative teaching, first that of a critical injection and, second, the development of critical partnerships. These actions didn't replace the technology of performativity but by reacting to the dominant performativity discourse and alternative initiatives available they forged a space for events that nurtured creative teaching and learning.

The first – a critical injection – was a dynamic and sudden intervention that interrupted the normal flow and threw it into sharp relief, a boost of energy that snapped people into action and creative fervour. The second – the development of critical partnerships – was the development of a relationship with specialist groups with a general interest in education but whose input created a source of creative energy for the teachers but that also affected the main pedagogic formats and systems.

The critical injection

As with the original critical events the two schools planned in detail, often, as in these cases, developing whole-school projects and gaining support from governors and parents. The critical injection was a visible disturbance of the highly systematised curriculum programme and of the routinised format of literacy and numeracy hours and set weekly timetables that have now come to dominate primary schools (Jeffrey 2002). They contrasted with the normal daily secure pattern of routines. They occupied specific dates in the school calendar for all to see and they raised the expectations of parents, students and governors as well as teachers similar to the Christmas show, sports day or the school play. They were seen to be significant meaningful events within the general curriculum programme (Jeffrey 2004).

The first school in our study – Suburbia – exemplified the critical injection approach. They planned a series of curriculum weeks over two years in which designated curriculum co-ordinators were allocated £700 to design a week of learning experiences focusing on their specific curriculum area and involving all the staff and with many external local contributions. They included multicultural, history, science, book, numeracy, design and technology, and PE weeks:

We've had these ideas in the past but we'd never been allowed to carry them through. We set up a designated 'weeks' budget. People were bubbling. These ideas that were under the surface before they were allowed to rise.

(Veronica, Head)

During a special maths week the whole school focused on pattern and shape and the maths co-ordinator arranged different specialist activities for different age groups within the school. Class teachers also designed specific programmes for their own class or collaboratively with other classes. Two classes visited Watford Football Club to carry out number crunching exercises, specialist PE teachers gave lessons on shape, two classes visited the local secondary school to use some of their maths apparatus, all the children took part in a sponsored 'mathelon' to raise money for the Great Ormond St Children's Hospital in London and they had a maths trail one afternoon where the classes moved around to every teacher carrying out a different maths activity in each classroom. The quality of learning was enhanced by the time available and the themed approach. 'There were more open-ended tasks, more problem solving, an opportunity to do different types of maths that don't really fit into what we have to do day by day. There was different lateral thinking' (Miriam, Yr5-T). This particular critical injection released teachers and students from the accountability of performance, reintroduced a theme-based curriculum, increased participative pedagogies, challenged professional norms and brought the community closer:

I'd love to see a primary school running like this the whole time. There has to be schemes of work and a National Curriculum but when I see some of those children lying on the floor building 3D mathematical structures my heart goes out to them because we are also going to put them under assessments, tests and yet they learn more in one morning here and are able to apply it to a situation than sitting there the whole term in the classroom.

(Veronica, Head)

Having 'a whole week with one focus, you feel freer' (Sally, Yr3-T). The boundaries were relaxed and 'you've no parameters so you stretch yourself. There's all this thinking outside the box and not being stuck with an idea but taking it one step further' (Cloe, Yr2-T).

It's a week where we can do what we want we think is OK. It doesn't matter if it doesn't work we try it out, whereas if you try that sort of thing in the normal weeks of school and it didn't work we'd get a backlash from it. So if it doesn't work, within the week you're not so worried.

(Cloe, Yr2-T)

The themed approach in conjunction with a whole week to carry out the project harked back to a more holistic approach to curriculum organisation, one in which 'you end up being more creative than you thought you were going to be on a Monday morning because you go with it, because you haven't got the time constraints' (Miriam, Yr5-T). Teachers were able to locate curriculum reference points in activities within the same week:

> I like all the different ideas. I liked the way they all linked together. Maybe something you've done on Monday will link into something you've done on Wednesday afternoon and they can link all those ideas together whereas usually what you're doing Monday morning is nothing to do with what you're doing Wednesday afternoon.
>
> (Sally, Yr3-T)

They provided rationales for any possible criticisms:

> If anyone says to me, 'when are you going to make up that time for the National Curriculum subjects?', I would say 'it's not necessary because it is cross-curricula'. The children were using thinking and applying numbers so I've more than covered my numeracy hour. The speaking and communication is covered and the children are writing up events using different forms of writing.
>
> (Veronica, Head)

The cross-curricula aspect allowed them to 'blend all the different subjects together. We felt as if we were in an investigation rather than a lesson' (Tracy, Yr5-T). This particular injection had enabled the more experienced teachers to create an opportunity for less experienced teachers to take part in a pedagogy experienced only by those who had taught prior to the National Curriculum.

Associated pedagogies and enhanced immersion in the curriculum (Woods 1993, 1995; Beetlestone 1998; Jeffrey and Woods 2003) resulted in a meaningful purpose rather than just meeting performance objectives:

> A fantastic week because it showed the link between learning and real life. We took one basic concept and spent most of the week doing it by drawing mats, nets, boxes and starting there. But we ended up hitting their history and art projects as well. You see this amazing mixture of skills and knowledge, which is life.
>
> (Miriam, Yr5-T)

Other advantages concerned the time made available for individual learners:

> When you have a whole week with children who work at a slightly slower pace they pick up more because they're able to repeat, re-visit in

a larger chunk of time. So they don't lose that bit in between, having to change to other subjects.

(Cloe, Yr2-T)

The time available allowed teachers to attend to individual needs:

If a child showed a spark of interest in a particular field then I nurtured it, whereas normally in our regimented tight curriculum you don't have that chance. You have more opportunity to see a different side to the children that you wouldn't normally see.

(Tracy, Yr5-T)

This approach also closed the gap between teacher and learner: 'Cross-curricula approaches allow your thoughts and the child's thoughts to go along the same path' (Miriam, Yr5-T).

These participative engagements involved assertions, debates, questions, critique, reflective observations, problem posing, possibility thinking and negotiations. They also involved empathy, consideration, relationship building, inclusion, emotional management and teamwork. Teachers and children joined together to investigate their themes, 'Often the children come up with ideas and spark off your ideas so you can take it one stage further and it's that spontaneity which helps the creativity' (Cloe, Yr2-T), developing their creative teaching and learning in the process. The focus on a shared engagement (Jeffrey and Woods 1997) inspired student initiative and, in some instances, developed student leadership:

One boy said, 'I'd like to show what I mean in a model, could I do a model?' 'Yes, please do it.' It was a fantastic three-dimensional model, which I couldn't have done. It inspired the other children, and took them in different directions because I had enough time to allow this to happen.

(Tracy, Yr5-T)

This particular example of injection of curriculum weeks meant extended professional challenges for those not particularly skilled in some subjects:

You feel far more confident about starting some weeks than others because of your own inhibition about different subjects. We've got a music week coming up, in the Spring Term, and I know that's going to challenge me because I'm not the most musical of teachers, so I will have to do something. But isn't that creativity – doing it my way?

(Cloe, Yr2-T)

The injection had an effect on the whole ethos:

Without any doubt it improved morale, enhancing teachers' leadership skills. Again they had to work together to plan. They see the mechanics of how it works, timetabling, sharing of jobs, meetings. You can see the results of the planning, teachers working together.

(Veronica, Head)

This critical injection was a shot to the system, a single event in a short space of time, an infusion of creativity that did not challenge the performativity discourse nor carried any danger of the school being penalised by inspectors. On the contrary, it added to the school's esteem to be seen energising learning while at the same time maintaining target imperatives. It was not meant to take on the powerful performativity discourse but to show parents, governors, friends and inspectors that alternative forms of curriculum organisation and pedagogy have advantages. In Suburbia's case it was an exemplar of what creative teaching and learning could look like and the meaning it could have for both teachers and students (Jeffrey 2004) using a cross-curricular approach wrapped in a subject-centred curriculum focus.

The school opened itself up to its own creativity:

> It gives me a huge amount of pleasure; the teachers held their heads up high, shoulders not down, everyone's happy. They haven't got the world on their shoulders and neither have the children and that has a knock-on effect. I just get excited at the thought that I've empowered someone to be able to lead a whole week in school. I've empowered them to communicate with other members of staff and with outside agencies, which is always good for us, and the children have got smiles on their faces.
>
> (Veronica, Head)

The relationship with the parents was different, they 'come in but they're not scrutinising how much time you spend on each subject' (Cloe, Yr2-T), but engaged with our curriculum week which further cemented the school's good relations:

> It was nice to emphasise to the parents that numeracy is fun and can be fun, not just about the formal recording of sums that some parents think it is. Maths is in fact about applying what you've got and being able to work in the real world, to help you out with problems in difficult situations, not just hundreds, tens, units. The week helped parents because they raised awareness of what we expected numeracy to be, what it looks like and what being numerate is.
>
> (Harriat, Foundation)

The week ended with a presentation of the week's activities and the explosion of activity reverberated across the county:

> We put an art gallery up for the parents at the same time as the Annual General Meeting. Parents came in through the door, they then stayed

for the meeting which used to be very low in numbers, so we really felt that we'd hit targets in so many different ways. Teachers were sent from other schools by their head teachers to find out what was going on at Suburbia, 'because we liked the sound of it'.

(Veronica, Head)

The reaction to the injection was that 'it was an incredible boost that we were grabbing back some of that creativity, some of that enthusiasm, what primary schools are all about' (Veronica, Head).

The effects of the injection on the teachers was to reinvigorate, on a regular basis, their creative teaching, to begin the process of amending the imposed mainstream pedagogies to incorporate creative teaching and learning and to redress their creative teaching experience. The effects

> raised the morale of the children who became quite excited and I got the impression that they're learning without knowing that they're learning. It became enjoyable, relevant rather than teaching by rote, it was actual hands on. They want to do the thing and then apply this knowledge and they don't realise how much they are learning [for the learners' perspectives, see Jeffrey 2004].
>
> (Charles, Governor)

A critical injection results in positive emotions, invigorated social relations, higher and more creative pupil achievement, and an increase in teacher professionalism and morale (Woods 1993). It inspires teachers with enthusiasm for a special event, gives them something to look forward to, and in particular something that is challenging the status quo. The injection is for all the school and therefore they are all affected by it and consequently it has a social dimension of collaboration with other teachers that is limited for the rest of the year. During the event learners and colleagues engage with a wide range of unusual and experimental pedagogies. There is a buzz in the school as a whole and in the staff room where excited voices can be heard describing the critical event in terms of learners' reactions and teacher dynamism.

There is a climax as the school reports the week to its constituents – in this case at a parents' meeting on the last day of the week. The following week the school settled back into 'normal' activity but some of the innovations of the event are reintroduced into the main pedagogy. As the routine of the term begins to dominate the teachers begin to look forward to the next injection and the possibility of working closely with other school or external colleagues. The fluid of the injection is never quite dissipated, and its effects linger on.

The educational gain for teachers is the construction of a solid base for being innovative. Learners are able to remind teachers of the way they felt invigorated during the event and of its positive effects in challenging any mutual intrumentalism (Pollard *et al.* 2000) likely to dominate in the face of any performativity discourses (Ball 1990). A constant confrontation emerges between the deadening hand of the 'delivery curriculum' (Dadds 1994) and the possibility of appropriation of national policies by creative teachers (Woods 1995).

Critical partnerships

One significant aspect of Suburbia's critical injection reported here was the involvement of external groups to enhance the event. The critical partnership at Tunnel School highlighted the full power of these relationships.

Schools, colleges and teachers, according to the UK seminar papers, developed strategic partnerships with national programmes, local groups, community operations and specialist consultants. The partnerships brought new ideas, perspectives, relationships and outcomes into the educational process. They took advantage of specific funded programmes such as the government-funded Creative Partnership Scheme and funds from Education Action Zones to increase their creative teaching opportunities by bringing in a host of local education projects, local experts and community groups to bolster the critical event. These were often part of a critical injection, but critical partnerships were longer-lasting interventions into the school's termly and annual curriculum plans. A critical partnership is incorporated over time and integrated into the existing timetable on a regular basis over a number of weeks or a term or even a year. Both the critical injection and the critical partnerships involved cross-curricula pedagogies and required a considerable effort of engagement with advisors, artists, specialist funders, workshop providers and project specialists.

One of the most significant aspects of these critical events for the learners was being part of a group exploration involving external experts, critical others (Woods 1995 and see Chapter 5) and project co-ordinators in which they took part in co-participative, collective and collaborative activity between adults and between adults and learners as well as between learners themselves (Jeffrey 2005). However, it is the adult partnerships that are the focus of this chapter. These partnerships conformed to a critical event in itself as the teachers became more involved with the external personnel and the latter became more involved with the school.

The second research site was a new school built on reclaimed land in an urban development near a major river crossing – Tunnel School – that had put creativity at its core by appointing a co-ordinator to develop the area across the school. Tunnel School had three significant partnership projects in operation during this research. The first involved a six-week partnership project between one Year 4 class and an artist specialising in Sounds in the Environment. The second was a four-year project with the National Theatre and the third was a playground development project – Grounded in Colour (GIC).

The significance of these partnerships for the recovery of creative teaching was in the common principles of teaching and learning established

between the partners which, at the same time, contrasted with each partner's different role, perspective, skill and experience.

Andrea, the creativity co-ordinator, met an artist on a course – Valerie –
who specialised in Sounds in the Environment. She felt that a project along
these lines might help re-establish some creative teaching. This particular
partnership developed from being part of a teacher–artist forum: 'There
were lots of common experiences between us in lots of different settings,
watching theatre being formed and discussions in interactive workshops
facilitated by other people' (Andrea, Yr4). She gained funds from the course
project to employ Valerie for a week's work spread over 4–5 weeks and they
spent many hours planning it:

> It gave us both faith in the project because we'd already developed that
> rapport. It was the first time for both of us on that course so there was
> a sense of journey for us in terms of taking it to children. She had an
> approach that wasn't that dissimilar to mine in that we wanted children
> to be as independent as possible. For instance a child asked 'What's the
> title?' and we both said 'What do you want it to be? You decide.' I
> think children respond brilliantly to adults that are obviously coming
> from the same place. There's normally only one teacher, there's never
> enough of you to go round, so if you have someone who's from the
> same kind of philosophy, you're underlining the project's importance,
> you're giving it higher status, you're able to reach more kids.
>
> (Andrea, Yr4)

The strength and depth of a partnership was a spur to creative action: 'It
was motivating and enthusing for me, as an adult, to have another adult
with me who's inspired by the content. That enthusiasm generates extra
enthusiasm' (Andrea, Yr4).

Their partnership involved creative evaluation, 'She'd notice things that I
didn't and vice versa and she'd had a conversation with a child that I hadn't,
so you'd got a double whammy going on there' (Andrea, Yr4), an aspect of
the authenticity provided by the critical other (Woods 1995, p. 97).

There is a developing dynamism for creative teaching and learning
through critical events which make it possible for the

> work to be organic, we haven't gone into any class and said this is what
> we're going to do. We've gone in and said 'What shall we do, what's
> possible?' The most successful projects have been the ones where we
> have had most time to focus on the design process, the investigation of
> ideas and themes and trips out to see other places. It added into this
> sense that we are all on a journey.
>
> (Sam, GIC)

This contrasts with the previous chapter which shows teachers creating
opportunities to manipulate a constraining curriculum on an everyday basis.

These critical partnerships are a juxtaposition of common philosophies but different lineages, expertise and crafts. In the National Theatre project a Year 5 class was involved in a 10-week project investigating Marlowe's play, *Faustus*. A musician/actor/educator carried out weekly workshops at the school over two terms for half a day a week and the final week consisted of a presentation of a short play at a local arts centre as well as a visit to the National Theatre to see a public performance of the play:

> I went to the Albany theatre and I was hugely impressed by the enthu-
> siasm and the expertise of the staff such as Kate – the artist – and the
> people who were leading it. So from the point of view of me it offered
> expertise that I couldn't deliver without investing a huge amount of
> time in preparing lessons and also knowledge as well. The artist came
> with a huge wealth of expertise in working with drama.
>
> (Graham, Yr5-DH-T)

The class tied the experience to a class project on the Tudors through visits to Tudor castles, finding out about Marlowe's life and visiting the place of his death – Deptford – putting character into the Tudor portraits they painted and discussing and writing about similar dilemmas across the ages: 'The Faustus project takes up a huge commitment of time but the benefits for the pupils are going to far out weigh the benefits of literacy and numeracy hours' (Graham, Yr5).

The artists acted as 'creative friends' as modelled in the Black Country Creative Partnership Evaluation report (Best *et al.* 2004) in which partner-ship development by artists is contextually, temporally and relationally dependent, rather than skills dependent. The report suggests that to be suc-cessful the creative 'friend needs to bring with them a bag of tricks, a passionate belief in creativity, an adaptable attitude, translation skills, and an ability to be both wily and willing' (ibid., p. 7). The third project exem-plified this differentiated but critical role. It was funded by £10,000 of government-funded Creative Partnership (CP) money to develop the school grounds to which the creativity co-ordinator had applied and been success-ful. This national £40 million CP programme was to encourage relations with the arts and especially community arts projects to assist the education of students in deprived areas. The school used the CP funds to employ a pro-ject artist and a sculptor over two terms to develop the grounds of the school – the Grounded in Colour (GIC) project – with all the classes in the school.

A critical partnership for this school, which was attempting to reintro-duce creative teaching, ensured that the relationships were differentiated but dynamic:

> Co-participation is a very dangerous way of working. It brings with it ter-
> rible problems and if you're a teacher working on a day to day basis it's a
> very scary thing to go into such a partnership. My job is to shake the box

and throw the rules out the window and it's my job to catch the bits when they fall. The teachers, as the process has gone on, have said, 'my God that was scary, you're mad for doing that', but they go with it because I'm experienced enough to go mad. A Yr3 teacher said the other day that my job is 'to come up with the biggest idea possible, go mad, and from that I, as the teacher, bring it down to something that's achievable'.

(Sam, GIC project worker)

To make such a partnership critical it is necessary to establish respect for each other:

I think there's a danger that artists are seen as the saviour of schools but I think teachers are incredibly creative. To take a curriculum with its restrictions and dullness and its demands and make that interesting on a day to day basis is very difficult. It's very easy in lots of ways for me to flit in, be exciting and go away again. I don't have to worry about kid's literacy progress etc. but they do.

(Sam, GIC)

These critical partnerships can only function in an authentic collaboration in which each other's independence is guaranteed and respected. What makes a critical partnership is the commitment of the artist or the interventionist to the partner as well as the partnership:

I would encourage the artist within the teacher. Frances, who is my partner teacher of the class, couldn't understand at first what I was doing. But when she took part in the sessions she felt that there was something a little bit more that she would like to get hold of. I'm not so interested to create art with the children, the main interest is that we are involved in the process, it has a beginning, middle and then you go to your class and do other things.

(Frank, GIC sculptor)

Although this close commonality in philosophy was central to the critical partnership so was a differentiated professional role:

The planning was a crucial thing and we spent quite a lot of time having conversations out of school, during the project as well. She might have an idea, like a concept that she would want to introduce to them, want them to explore and then I'd come along with how it could be made accessible by the children, how to keep it learner friendly if you like.

(Andrea, Yr4)

As with the critical injection, the professionalism of the teachers is enhanced through the partnership as their different roles are exposed:

We can learn so much from having workshops and it's been fantastic that we have got Creative Partnerships here but the important thing is that we're in the position to make the decision ourselves about what we want to happen. This is our school, this is our identity, we are a group of professionals, this is our development plan, these are our priorities and CP helps us to get there with quality and excitement.

(Andrea, Yr4)

As with Hackleton in Chapter 8, these creative developments were welcomed by Ofsted, and thus constitute a reconstruction of the discourse of performativity, showing learning to be broader and more meaningful than how it was constrained to be in the first manifestation of that discourse:

Teachers make good use of the local environment as starting points for teaching pupils about what affects the local area and what can be done to improve it … Staff encourage pupils' creative skills and this is reflected in high quality art and display work. The school is a 'Creative Partnership School' and resident artists inspire the children they work with.

(Andrea, Yr4)

At the same time they maintained the technology of the performativity programme and 'improved achievement levels as measured by SATs from the last inspection' (Andrea, Yr4).

Conclusion

These schools showed that they could challenge the dominant discourse by taking up alternative discourses bolstered by government support. They were seizing an initiative that was spreading across primary schools to introduce curriculum weeks as special events involving the community and parents. This kind of initiative played well with Ofsted and the government who were keen for schools to be responding to local interests as well as meeting standards agendas. Ofsted reports praised these community initiatives focused on learning based on the government's aim of encouraging excellence and enjoyment (DfES 2003a). Heads and teachers realised that this was, hopefully, a thin edge of the wedge in which they would begin to integrate the curriculum more often, returning to project work approaches favoured prior to the National Curriculum's introduction. They also used the funds and work of Creative Partnerships to establish longer cross-curricula projects, again gaining support from Ofsted for such innovative initiatives. These are examples of agency working with and against the superstructure to develop creativity teaching and learning. However, schools still have to work with standards agenda and the performativity imperatives of government and the next case study is an example of one such school whose teachers manage this difficult operation.

8 Reintroducing creativity
Becoming a 'Particularly Successful School'

Introduction

In the last two chapters we have been considering how schools, particularly those stuck in the performativist quagmire, become creative or rediscover the creativity they once had. In this chapter, we trace what has been happening over the last ten years in one school which shows the whole career of a journey from the practices associated with one discourse to those associated with another. Year by year, from heavily constrained beginnings, there has been a steady development in creative teaching and learning in the school to its position today as an 'Innovative Practice Partnership' (IPP) school and one of Ofsted's 'Particularly Successful Schools'.

Hackleton is a rural primary catering for some 209 pupils aged 4 to 11. It is in mainly, though not exclusively, a middle class area, and there are no children currently eligible for free school meals. About 10 per cent are on the school's special educational needs register. There are eight full-time teachers and three teaching assistants. Teacher turnover and rates of unauthorised absence among the children are low.

Hanging on

Things were most difficult at the school from the point of view of creative teaching at about the time of the introduction of the literacy hour in 1998. Teachers' difficulty is illustrated by their attempt to hang on to some vestiges of creativity, notably in the biennial trip of Years 5 and 6 to the Isle of Wight towards the end of every other summer term. One of us accompanied them in 2000. It seemed to the researcher that the week was caught between two ideologies, ministering to teacher-directiveness in some aspects, but acting in a spirit of creative activity in others.

Amongst the former, there was the heavy directiveness of some of the local presenters giving talks on some of the places of interest visited, as contrasted with the 'critical others' in the 'critical events' mentioned in Chapter 7. Second, the activity afterwards, where the children prepared personal folders on the week, seemed largely teacher-directed. The Literacy Strategy was a strong influence. Children, for example, were encouraged to write a 'recount', a rather formalised record of the week, and to compose a story based on their visit to *HMS Victory*, but to a given structure. There were no free-writing personal diaries. Nothing in the folders captured what a wonderful, exciting, critical event it was for them. In discussions with the researcher they had plenty to say on this score. Clearly the week scored strongly on citizenship, on relationships, and as an aid to the transition from primary–secondary; junior–senior; child–adult. They also made some mature and constructive critique of some of the talks they had listened to – all positive gain and, one might argue, worthy of written record. The one creative exercise was one of persuasive writing, at which there was considerable ingenuity, suggesting what might have been achieved elsewhere.

This is not to demean the results of the week, which were considerable and positive; nor to criticise the teachers. It demonstrates, rather, how activities were inhibited by National Curriculum requirements; and by the sheer pressures on teachers and pupils alike which had them exhausted long before the end of term. Standards in academic subjects were also not high when the Head at the time first came to the school. They steadily rose, however, under his stewardship, giving them the confidence soon to make a bold move.

Day 10

The origins

The idea came to the Head in his bath one morning.

The creative arts, which he and his colleagues championed as being of key significance in the education of young people, were not well served by the National Curriculum (NACCCE 1999). The school now had the buffer of good SATs results and a recent good Ofsted inspection in 1999. So now why shouldn't the teachers take the initiative and devote some time to the promotion of the arts? It would help promote the basic school aim: 'To provide the best quality education possible, giving experience of excellence, in a happy, caring environment.'

It was in the spirit of this aim that the teachers instituted a 'creative arts' morning, to be held on every other Friday during the school year 2000–1 ('Day 10'). The specific aims according to the staff were to:

1 return high status to the arts within the school curriculum;
2 redress the curriculum balance with regard to the domination of literacy and numeracy;
3 develop creativity and thinking skills;
4 develop children's fine motor skills;
5 develop collaborative learning across children of all year groups;
6 enjoy the arts.

So the Head and staff instituted a new session into the fortnightly timetable, whereby every other Friday morning the normal curriculum was abandoned in favour of the creative arts. Staff volunteered their own activities. The children were divided into mixed age groups of about 20 in number and spent a whole morning on one activity, moving around each fortnight from session to session, to drama and dance (a play based on the story of St George and the Dragon), mask-making, weaving, marbling, bubble painting, collage, music and composition, percussion, rainforest painting – the menu for that particular year.

The idea of a Day 10 is not new. It was first used by secondary schools in the 1970s to provide some variety in the rigid timetable (see, for example, Fletcher *et al.* 1985). It is an interesting commentary on recent developments that it should now reappear in a primary school. It might be seen as an attempt to recapture some of the elements of child-centred and discovery learning (Sugrue 1997), underwritten by constructivist learning theory (Vygotsky 1978), so vilified and squeezed by governments since the late 1980s (Campbell 1993a; Woods *et al.* 1997; Triggs and Pollard 1998). It is also a form of adaptation to the escalation of pressures on teachers and their time, the almost exclusive focus on measurable performance, and the downgrading of the artistic and affective side of teaching and learning which has characterised government policy since the late 1980s (Apple 1986; Hargreaves 1994; Ball 1998). Further, it offers an opportunity for teachers to regenerate their own sense of professionalism (Woods and Jeffrey 1996; Osborn *et al.* 2000).

We evaluated this scheme after its first year, using qualitative methods in the attempt to discover reactions, understand experiences, and to uncover some of the rich detail of the interaction (Hitchcock and Hughes 1995). A democratic model of research was adopted wherein the perspectives of all involved were sought, and conclusions fed back into the school's policy-making framework (MacDonald 1975; Walker 1989). The following account draws on talks with the Head, Rob Breeze, members of staff, children and parent-governors; observations by researchers of four sessions, at the end of the summer term; and written evaluations by Class 6 children and the teachers.

Educational benefits

Positive emotions

Day 10 revived the old feelings of 'pedagogical magic' and 'love of learning', inducing positive emotions like warmth, enjoyment, self-confidence, and pride in one's work. Positive emotions flowed from the general school climate. Rob drew attention to the quality of artwork and display. Display is about the 'ethos and culture that we wish to project to the wider world. And it just makes the environment nicer, which is also important for the children, and the staff who work in it':

Display sets the tone, and it values the children's work. It gives them pride in seeing their work on walls. It's a great pleasure for children to see their work displayed. You see photographs of things we've done, and children will look at them thinking 'Yes, there I am. I remember doing that', even though they've been up for some time. It's that kind of thing that reinforces their personal history within the school. It's motivational and good PR.

There is a very distinctive climate during these Friday sessions. Two parent governors who spent a whole morning there wrote a letter of appreciation to the Head in which they said, 'We left with what can only be described as a warm glow.' The researcher also felt this late during his first morning, when, having visited most of the activities, he found himself standing in the main corridor studying the wall display. He could hear the percussionists, some background music from the play in the hall, a modulated babble of sound from the bubble painting room, and more distant noises from the masks and weaving activities. There was a sense of the whole school being engrossed in creative exercise. Similarly, when the activities finished and children returned to their own classrooms carrying their products with them, there was a buzz of excitement as they shared their experiences. They were even heard talking about art, dance, music, etc. in the playground.

These activities reassert that learning is not just a matter of painful toil, but can be fun. Enjoyment was evident at every turn:

I would hate children to leave this school and, when they look back, think what we did was literacy and numeracy. What I remember of my school days was the creative things ... (Rob)

The most important thing is that they had fun. (Class 6 pupil talking of other pupils)

In the various classrooms, children were all demonstrably enjoying themselves. They were doing something new to them, not the sort of thing they would do at home like drawing or crayoning. One child commented that he had broadened his knowledge: 'I know more elements of art rather than just painting.'

Teachers create climates of anticipation, expectation and excitement (Woods and Jeffrey 1996). This was especially noticeable in the drama. There was an air of anticipation evident in the very early stages. This was something 'unusual'. What was going to happen? What were they going to be required to do? The teacher sets the scene, introducing them to the concept of 'exaggerated movements' through a brief activity involving receiving a present in a parcel delivered by the postman. The group stands watching, quietly observing whilst the teacher demonstrates receiving her present. The atmosphere is charged with anticipation. The children do not know what to expect. There is no routine here. One can almost hear the children asking 'What is going to happen here?' Again, later, there is an air of excitement as they await the arrival of the 'audience' who are going to view the finished play.

The teachers also enjoy the activities, and their enjoyment is sometimes infectious, as the following fieldnotes demonstrate:

In the drama, Jo Roberts exudes confidence and all can see and feel that she is having a wonderful time as she prepares the ground. Then, 'Mrs Roberts has to keep quiet now.' The activity becomes theirs, and they take over with equal enthusiasm. Every child, irrespective of age, feels that they are part of the team. There seemed a total lack of self-consciousness amongst them, no sense of inferiority, or 'I am unable to perform this task'. In effect, the drama seemed to release their best efforts. For example, bigger boys in the drama performed some very graceful movements. They might have been more self-conscious in other situations. Equally, the way a small girl responded with her partner in the early stages of the drama gave her confidence to take part fully. She was told, 'You were so good!' Asked by the researcher if she enjoyed doing this, her face broke into a big smile and she said, 'Yes, I lubbit!' In marbling, there is an atmosphere of feverish excitement in the room as the group complete their books. Helen shows me hers proudly. What is she going to do with it? She is going to take it home and write in it. Hannah wrote later that 'marbling was good fun and an amazing effect. I was very proud with my books which I had made in the morning.' As I leave the marbling group, the teacher remarks, 'It's lovely to see them all like this, enjoying themselves.'

When Denise's own class returns, they sit on the floor to show and explain excitedly to each other what they have been doing. Jamie explains how, with Miss Lett, they had to get different coloured paper, dip it in paints ...

Rhiana did a butterfly with Miss Heden, three girls explaining the intricacies of collage. Callum was in Miss Knight's. He made three butterflies then a lion ... made its mane and tail with a sponge because it looked like fun. He did it yellow, with brown on top, with little rollers, and then a border.

All talk very enthusiastically about what they have been doing, some descriptively and at length. There is carry-over beyond school. A parent told how her little boy looked forward to 'art day'. She doesn't want her child dominated by SATs. She thinks they should do more of Day 10 work. Her child in Year 6 brings things home, and is very proud of the things he has made, hangs them up around the house, and is talking about it for the rest of the week.

Social relationships

At a macro level there are signs of a school and a community bonding. The mixed age groups added a longitudinal level to the existing horizontal one. Rob thought, 'There were benefits not just inside the school, but in the playground, and I'm sure outside the school as well.' A number of parent-governors assisted voluntarily in the activities. Other adults, such as the lunchtime assistants, were drawn in also (as audience for the play in their case). As the researcher leaves the marbling group, he is thanked for coming in. By observing the marbling, he's been joining in with it. All are welcome.

Teamwork is paramount. Some of the activities – the drama, the music activities – involve the product of a joint effort. In drama especially, the group developed a strong feeling of working together. No one wanted to let the team down. Despite the age differences, they were all equal partners in this enterprise. And they accepted the teacher's advice or criticism like professionals.

In music and composition, groups had to compose a verse, illustrate it, and set it to music. There was much experimentation and serious discussion:

> 'How about if Tom [Class 6] and I go in the middle and you two go last?'
> Tom allocates parts ... 'and you two do the singing as well ...'
> 'OK, get ready you three ...' He counts them in, '1, 2, 3 ...'
> 'Now let's all do the singing ...' (Fieldnote)

Where a class was divided into groups, there was still a sense of co-operation among, rather than competition between, the groups. In the music and composition class, for example, the groups were arranged in a circle for the performances, so they could all see each other, and take part in each other's performances. All join in the singing of each group's verse. Denise ensures all participate, giving especial attention to the youngest. Some are timid on their instruments at the first attempt. 'Rebecca [Yr1], did you play yours?' They do it again, much better, and we all applaud. Rebecca is pleased. Denise brings the little ones into the community often with a personal comment that shows she esteems the child as an individual at the same time. She is liberal with her praise: 'Tom, you kept time beautifully, well done! It's not easy to keep the beat! Do they get a thumbs or a [indicates thumbs down]?' Of course, it is thumbs up. There is no sense of one group being better than another. They are all good in their own terms, with the class as a whole doing the evaluation.

The most notable feature was the extent of learning amongst the children from the interaction. The children were urged to discuss ideas amongst themselves: Sylvia Newnham urges, 'Talk to a partner, that always helps ... If you can't draw, Mrs Heden or I will help you.' Particularly noticeable here was the way in which older children aided younger. There were many examples of this. In general, teachers suggested that the older ones might help in this way, but they chose if, when and how they did it.

Older children sometimes learnt from younger. The youngest in a group sometimes provided the basic idea for the group's activity. Thus, in one group in musical composition, Sophie (Class 1) had the main idea for their verse: 'The ants go marching three by three, the little one stopped to have some tea.' This was then illustrated and set to music by the whole group. The following fieldnotes give examples of interactive teaching and learning:

> Jade (Yr6) is assisting several younger children in bubble painting: 'Choose what colour basket you want. Do you want this? Or this?' She tells another little girl to 'Come here', patting a seat beside her. 'Do you know where your balloon is? Shall we start another colour, because you only have three? Did you want blue, or red?' Jade seems in charge of the whole table. 'Yours is coming on, Victoria.'

Working with children of all ages, and especially younger children, was the most gratifying aspect of the activities for Class 6 children. They enjoyed it because 'I wasn't very confident before' ... 'I liked helping to encourage them to think of their own designs' ... 'they can ask you for your help, so you know that they can trust you, and it might encourage them to help other people when they're in Year 6' ... 'you were working with different teachers in different classrooms'.

Here we see some good examples of 'scaffolding' – the process of propping up a child's learning until it is internalised and the child can use the knowledge on his or her own (Bruner 1986). But there are also beneficial educational reverse effects for the older children, improving social skills, bringing intrinsic rewards, and raising confidence and self-esteem.

Pupil achievement

The activities gave free rein to pupil creativity, the extent of which was a revelation to teachers. One teacher thought the 'end products were better and better as the weeks progressed'. Sue Roberts wondered where their conceptualisation comes from. Do they see it when they start? Does it develop? At what point? Sue thinks adults are more constrained, and hidebound by phobias. Children are more open and adventurous, more prepared to take risks, and to play. The activities offer the children an increased range of opportunities for them to express, develop and discover skills and abilities. It's about giving them confidence and letting them loose. They liked it 'because the teacher doesn't take that long to explain' ... 'you get in a big mess and it's a case of experimenting' ... 'you have a lot of fun' ... 'you get to be really creative'.

A multitude of skills are involved. For example, in drama and dance, the researcher noted 'the level of memory retention required is high – there are quite complex patterns and sequences. All the children, regardless of age, were able to remember and enact the necessary sequences.' Other skills included: creativity, body movement/control/dance, musical sensitivity, emotional awakening and sustainment, co-operation/sharing, a blend of individual and joint responsibility, musical timing, translation of fantasy/ legend/history, and relating to real life.

Activity-based work gives children the opportunity to appreciate authorship from the inside. For example, from the drama, children can develop a new sense of what 'drama' can mean by their participation and performance to an audience, giving new insights into its powers of expression and emotional involvement. The initial session was fairly contrived, but as the lesson progressed, body movements and facial expressions became more expressive. They were coming from *within*, rather than from, for example observations of TV. The teacher said, 'Now the townspeople have to be frightened of this dragon', and they all gave a wonderful display of fear … Later, the teacher called upon the children in the final scenes to 'become the dragon'. 'Use your eyes, hands and bodies to become this frightening creature.' There was an uninhibited response from both boys and girls – an example of how gender, as well as age, lines are crossed at times in these activities.

There are orchestrating skills, most noticeably in music. 'Now put down your instruments. We've had the thinking, the drawing, the writing, the experimenting …' Now comes the performance, with the rest of the class as the audience, arranged in a circle so they can all see each other. But 'putting things together' applied to other activities too, for example bubble painting, which was 'in two parts – a balloon bit and then the bubbles, and then you have to put it all together'.

Some children discovered hidden talents. Oliver, not generally recognised as an artist, made a brilliant bicycle in collage. Hannah's snail in collage was the 'best piece of artwork I have ever done. I have improved my artwork a lot more and I'm happy about that as I've never trusted myself in art and I do now as I think I'm better.' Frazer had become 'more imaginative in my designs'. Charlie in Class 1 surprised his teacher with the clarity of his lines in his mask of a monster. Kim Heden was also surprised, especially by boys. 'You don't think of collage as a boy's activity', but a number had done brilliant work. Sue says, 'They come up with some really good ideas.'

There were some brilliant results in artwork, but it was not always easy to explain how they were achieved. Often it was a case of defying the rules and repeated experimentation. 'How did you design yours?' 'I did lines like that.' 'Why is this line in beans?' 'I just did it like that.'

It seems necessary to make the resources available, explain the object of the activity, and show a few basic techniques to get them started. The same applies to collage. Kim doesn't want to restrict the children. They need their freedom. She wants them to develop an image in their own mind, and then find the resources to do it, rather than be constrained by the resources that are available (though they are multifarious in her room – suggestive rather than constraining – all sorts of pasta, beans, peas, rice, sticky paper in different colours, crêpe paper, cotton wool, sand, shells, magazines, cardboard, buttons, corks, etc. – and, of course, glue). Kim, who wants them to think about how things feel as well as how they look, introduces them to a wide range of examples. Among the completed collages were a saxophone, a sea scene, fireworks, a jungle scene, a race track, name plaques, a little sister, a garden scene (with clouds and rainbow), a horse and stables, a coelacanth, Thunderbirds, football shirts, a colourful wriggly snake (interestingly textured with scrunched-up crêpe paper) … Here is a desert scene by Tom, with sun, glaring sand, cactus; here a dinosaur, a T Rex … 'This shows where the meteorite hit … This is ancient England …' Symbolically, children are allowed to dress in what they like today, notionally to support a charity. But it helps to mark the day out as different, adding to their sense of individuality, and that the activities belong to them as individual persons, rather than to some externally prescribed model of pupil.

Teacher professionalism and morale

Teachers have a degree of freedom they do not have elsewhere in the curriculum. They generate their own activities. They go to Rob and say, 'I have an idea for next time …' Democracy prevails – amongst teachers and children. The idea of a Day 10 was discussed amongst the staff, and they volunteered suggestions. Some had to learn themselves, and there is a sense of all learning together. There is a degree of self-renewal here (Woods 1995). Denise says it reminds her of things she used to do and enjoy in her earlier years of teaching. She considers it the children's 'entitlement'. One of the great joys is that of working together – all ages and both sexes – and teachers too have a great collaborative sense. It 'rejuvenates' the staff. Denise gets up in the morning and thinks, 'Oh good, this is creative arts day.' Teachers contrast some other, 'nose to the grindstone', days (usually Mondays). The pressures are incessant, particularly this [summer] term, with SATs, report writing, parents' evening … a very heavy schedule. Day 10 is such a wonderful restorative.

Elsewhere in the week, Rob rearranged the morning schedule to fit things in. Numeracy and literacy used to take the whole morning. But Rob now brought the morning break forward, yielding an extra half an hour afterwards wherein they could do history and geography, more subjects that had been squeezed in the National Curriculum. This is an illustration of how tight things are. There is 'not enough time to draw breath'. 'Sometimes we have to say "Stop!" and we have to do what is best for these children in our immediate setting, and if there's a need we have to address it.' Day 10 has to be seen against this background of unrelenting pressure. Denise remarked how much more flexible she was over the literacy hour, compared to the early stages when she was quite rigid. So some space was being found elsewhere for teacher creativity. Day 10 must have aided this process.

In the drama and dance activity, it clearly required a strong and talented teacher to draw from the children the very best in creative terms. Huge amounts of initiative and energy were required, in which teachers expressed their own creativity. Teachers and children both became caught up in the activity as a unit, not as teacher transmitting a body of knowledge or skills to pupils. Teachers, perhaps, felt a sense of freedom, and a sense that they were contributing and sharing some of their own expertise which they considered of value but which was not valued in formal requirements. They were also able to practise the kind of constructivist, scaffolding pedagogy basic to their preferred child-centred learning. Sue commented, 'We don't teach', meaning 'we don't instruct'. But there was plenty of guidance, advice, illustration, stimulation, encouragement, enthusing and inspiring. Also, teachers were able themselves to evaluate the relative 'success' of a particular session, which must contribute to a sense of self-worth. One teacher said she felt 'enormous satisfaction and pride in the work produced by the children'.

Review

After a year, the teachers might claim that a start had been made on aims 1 and 2 (as specified in the introduction), though there was still a long way to go, and, arguably, ultimately required some relaxation of government pressure, if not their support and encouragement. There is a sense in which balance can only be achieved when the evaluation and assessment of creative arts activities is given equivalent status to the rest of the curriculum, and/or when it permeates that curriculum in meaningful ways. There had been some clear progress on aims 3 and 4, sufficient to surprise and delight the staff and to cause them to consider how they might take these further (see below). But the clearest achievements had been in aims 5 and 6, which might be regarded as a necessary first step, since they are conduits to the other four aims.

Pupil and teacher evaluation revealed that a big problem was time. The spirit of Day 10 seems to be with 'going with the flow' (Woods and Jeffrey 1996), but the structure leant more towards 'getting done', i.e. getting tasks completed in the time allocated.

How, too, did it relate to the National Curriculum? Was it just a bit of fun and relaxation as a reward for doing the 'proper' work well? But even the first Day 10 was not altogether out of line with official developments. A number of key skills in the National Curriculum were involved, such as team working, problem solving and communicating. But the staff thought they could do even better. They had made a start on the road back to the kind of teaching that they firmly believed promoted the best kind of learning. They now had to take it further. A useful resource from outside was at hand.

Artsmark (2001–2)

As an aid to meeting some of these perceived requirements, the staff decided to apply for an Artsmark award from the Arts Council of England – an example of a Creative Partnership. Artsmark aims to encourage schools to raise the standard of the arts and to raise the profile of arts education across the country. Some of the options in the scheme are 'developing cross-art form work to enhance pupils' understanding and experience of at least two different art forms'; 'using the arts to develop a creative approach to learning in other curriculum areas'; 'using ICT to enhance the delivery of the arts curriculum'. Other opportunities encouraged within lesson time include arts weeks, school productions, festivals and visits to arts venues, or by arts organisations, and visits to and partnerships with arts practitioners and arts organisations. Schools need to share and celebrate pupils' creative achievements within the whole school environment, and in the community. Regular provision of out-of-hours sessions are also required. Schools need to have appropriate professional development opportunities for their teachers. In these ways, the Artsmark award offered a structure, additional incentive, and foci for the next stage of Hackleton's regeneration of the arts, and for advancing the ambitious aims they had set themselves.

This phase was marked by these developments:

- A widening and deepening of creative practice. This applied across the curriculum. Links were forged between other subjects and the arts. For example, the teaching objectives and activities for the National Literacy Strategy for one week (involving spelling, punctuation, adjectives, etc.), using a story as a basic resource, shows how role-play, drama and art feed creativity and promotes the literacy objectives and literary appreciation. The teacher used subtle questioning – sparking the imagination, suggesting things to think about, drawing attention to subtle details in the text, encouraging the children to read and interpret the story creatively, taking it over, owning it. What do you think this is about? Where is it going next? What is she feeling? It is very carefully planned and the literacy objectives are worked in, in context.

- Extended connections outside the school. Links were forged with the Quantum Theatre for Science, Aesop's Touring Theatre Company, dance groups and visiting artists. The school used the local art gallery and museum facilities, and took part in special historical days.

- More thought, planning and system going into creative practice. There were whole focus days at the start of each term; a clear and comprehensive statement of policy. ('The arts give our children opportunities to explore their feelings, increase their knowledge, develop their skills and realise their aspirations; they provide ways of knowing, representing, interpreting and symbolising, and a context for appreciating and valuing; contact with the arts requires the ability to question, explore, collaborate and extend and develop one's ideas and the ideas of others.')

- More depth, complexity and variety. The inter-relating of curriculum areas and the application of skills gained in one situation to problems in another consolidates and extends skills and knowledge. It can be compared to the research technique of triangulation. Where a variety of methods, people, places, resources, skills, applications, etc. are being brought to bear on the same issue, it arguably heightens, deepens, enriches and confirms knowledge. It also, arguably, aids concept and theory formation. In seeing that the same phenomenon applies in different circumstances we begin to rise above the particular instance and understand abstract concepts. The recently installed ICT suite had considerable impact here.

- Day 10 was geared more closely into the school's curriculum. Its content was to be determined by the school's improvement plan. In its second year, it was felt that a focus on multiculturalism was needed in the school generally. As well as large-scale celebrations of all the religious festivals, therefore, Day 10 offered activities such as making kente cloths; Ojibwe/Chippewa Indian dream catchers; African Asimevo cloths; Rangoli patterns; and lotus flowers/dance. Sessions were also extended to two half days, so children could learn techniques on the first occasion and apply them on the second. Enthusiasm ran as high as ever.

- Sustained and more confident momentum. Other schools had become interested in Day 10 and Hackleton had a number of visitors. The Head received several invitations to speak in other schools. Artsmark provided a further goal, and when a gold award was made, that gave teachers a further boost. An invitation to contribute to a QCA video on creativity the following year confirmed their status now as a leading creative school and their own conviction that they were doing things 'right'.

Teachers still felt that the curriculum was being taught in an over-compartmentalised way. The achievement of being awarded an Artsmark Gold gave Hackleton the confidence to extend creativity into the rest of the curriculum. There now followed a major, full-scale reorganisation of the curriculum into 'Curriculum Flows'. Day 10 might have appeared at the beginning as only partially relating to the school's main work. But this next development brought everything together into a unified whole.

Curriculum Flows (2002 onwards)

Dawn, the current Head, had devised Curriculum Flows in her previous school and had been developing them here:

> We wanted a curriculum that we weren't looking at timetables thinking, 'Have I done my hour literacy? Have I done my hour numeracy here? And have I done my hour of science?' We wanted a curriculum where all of the subjects are intertwined.

Dawn argued that in general life circumstances we don't think in compartmentalised fashion but 'have to pull ideas and skills from everything that we've learnt'. In traditional teaching:

> We send them into Year 1 and say, 'Right, stop thinking for yourselves – we are now going to talk to you and that's how you're going to learn' and actually we've got a class full of young thinkers who can use their creative skills and their ideas to enhance their curriculum ... So that's how the curriculum flows came about ... We looked at all of the QCAs that we were teaching in school and very quickly we realised that the history subjects were the ones that could create the single field of study for us ... When we were learning about the Tudors we could look into science about keeping warm – how did the Tudors keep warm? The Tudor clothing, we could look in one of the art topics in Year 4 – portraits – Tudor portraits. When we researched even further we worked out that Michelangelo was born within that time, we could look at his portraits, and we can make out photo frames that we needed to in DT because we can put our Tudor portraits into them ...

The rationale was formalised into an official school document:

> Curriculum flows offer rich and exciting programmes of learning that give cohesion, meaning and motivation, harnessing the creativity, curiosity and energy of young people. The flows pull learning into a single field of study and a therefore understandable unity. They enable classroom environments to become focused centres of learning, and with such a shared focus between year groups and key stages, enable the whole school to become a learning zone for all children and staff.
>
> By linking subjects, timetabling the required curriculum to be covered is simple. There is more time for children to gain hands-on experiences, have more problem solving/research tasks and therefore learn in greater depth. Facts learned are anchored to meaning and have definite relationships with each other. There is 'learner centred learning'. Pupils work in teams, exploring and helping one another while the teacher sets directions, offers opportunities and acts as a guide and resource. The children ask better questions, seek their own answers and gain deeper insights than they had before.
>
> In addition to the traditional '3 Rs', this type of curriculum therefore also offers an additional '3 Rs': Research (searching out information); Reasoning (processing information); and Recording (creating a way to save and/or share information). In today's world, the body of knowledge is so large and the pace of acquisition so rapid that we must constantly change our teaching methods to prepare pupils for their life as adults. We must emphasise the higher levels of critical thinking:

Analysis: the ability to break down material into its component parts so its structure can be understood; Synthesis: the ability to put parts together to form a new whole; Evaluation: the ability to judge the value of material for a given purpose. Integrating these 'thinking skills' into our curriculum flows also enables children to take charge of their own learning, something they are naturally driven to do. (See Table 8.1.)

In summary, curriculum flows (all quotes from an interview with Dawn, HT):

• Integrate the compartmentalised National Curriculum, including literacy and numeracy, showing relationships and patterns in knowledge and systems. They also provide a focus for learning.

• Through this connectedness, encourage an emotional response in children which induces deeper learning. ('Any type of emotional response to a situation we know makes the learning go into the long-term memory. The only things I myself remember from school are situations like these. I remember one teacher who taught us everything through music, like the Exhibition of 1851 or the wives of Henry VIII through a song – a fantastic learning opportunity. I don't remember many things I learned in secondary school, but I remember being in Mr Frost's class.')

• Have 'enjoyment' as an aim for both pupils and teacher. ('We all enjoy our teaching more because we feel there's more excitement about the curriculum and there's more of a buzz around the school. Even walking up and down the corridor now – you can see and feel the whole school connected in their learning.' 'If the children know that I enjoy what I'm doing then they'll enjoy it more. If I can connect my learning and teaching throughout the flow and I can see a flow through, then I enjoy my teaching more and the children can connect their learning through the flow.')

• Have clear objectives and structures, while allowing scope for spontaneity and pupil initiative, imagination and creativity. ('I think it's very important to remember in any activity that there is a clear learning objective that you need the children to reach, but also that we must not stifle the children. We have to steer them to where we want them to go but if other learning opportunities come up within that lesson then we must go with them and we must actually stand back, take a deep breath and let the children have a go. But as far as steering them goes, you do want them to achieve, *they* want to achieve and you do want them to get to that end learning objective.')

• Encourage discovery. ('Why would you have to give a learning objective within the first five minutes of every lesson for every subject? Aren't some lessons a discovery thing first, before you say to the children, "Oh, wow, look we've made this and learnt this"? Don't you take away the creativity and the awe and wonder of it if you say, "Oh by the way, in half an hour this is going to blow up and great sparks are going to come out of it, but let's start now"? You don't do that ... children learn best by seeing it in practice when things link together. But we still do teach those odd lessons of skills that need to be taught, those lessons that just don't fit in, those things that are important and need to be taught as a separate lesson.')

- Draw upon a range of skills and previous experience. Encourage involvement. Children bring everything they know to their learning. ('Mine have been driving me mad all week 'cos I said we were going to be making these two walls, and we're going to be painting them and they keep asking me "Is it two walls today?" and we always do art on a Thursday, and on Tuesday they say, "I've brought my box, can we do it today – no we do art on Thursday ... can we start it now then ... we're going to cut up the boxes today and then we'll paint them tomorrow afternoon ... why can't we do it this afternoon ... because you have French and music don't you ... well can we do it in the morning ... I've drawn mine at home five times and changed it! ... so that's why we don't do things straight away, to give you some planning time ... but I'm so excited and want to do it ... but it's tomorrow now, that's all you've got to think, you've only got to wait till tomorrow." So they're driving me to distraction and I think isn't it a good thing to tell them so far in advance! So that was a good example 'cos James has drawn his now five times at home and someone has been on the Internet to find out what plaster of Paris actually was, they said it looks very messy ... So the fact that they look at things like this means the children revisit things very, very often, through research. They say if you don't talk about things five times it doesn't stay in your memory at all.')

- Focus on experiential learning. ('Children need to experience what is happening. If you don't ask them how they feel being there, then that goes back to our old style of teaching where I just read it from a book and they don't have to think about how they felt. It's vitally important that children share their emotions.')

- Provide authenticity to learning. ('If they didn't complete that log today they wouldn't be able to make their hospital. There was an actual real learning intention that they needed to do before moving on and it makes the learning real for them. Why are we learning about number bonds in numeracy? Because you're going to be able to complete your log in history. Why are we learning about how to use drawing tools in ICT? Because you're going to make a floor plan of Scutari Hospital. Not because I want you to aimlessly sit there making boxes on the computer screen and filling them with colours.')

- Flow across the whole school, integrating knowledge at various levels. For example, 'Children in Year 2 learning about Florence Nightingale are linked to children in Year 6 who are learning about the Victorians. Year 2 have turned their classroom into a Florence Nightingale museum which Year 6 then visits. Year 2 have also written a book about Mary Seacole based on their researches and this will be a resource for next year's Year 2 – an added purpose for the children writing it.' 'Reading conferencing' during the research stage also brings older and younger children together, the latter receiving invaluable aid, the former also learning and growing in maturity as they become more skilled in handling the groups in child-centred ways.

- Require a range of quality resources to stimulate children's minds and provide scope for experimentation. This includes a range of basic and fairly cheap items – textiles, paints, glues, instruments, papers, fastenings, etc.; as well as more sophisticated and expensive ones such as ICT, media suites, and interactive white boards.

- Create time. The work on Florence Nightingale, for example, allows more time to learn more facts about Florence than those specified in the National Curriculum, to include the Victorians and Mary Seacole. And it only takes half a term rather than a whole term as formerly.

- Create space. 'The whole school environment – classrooms, corridors, other rooms, playgrounds, fields, etc. – should be a learning zone for the children, not just the classroom.' Corridor displays, for example, all have a theme. 'The work that's on the displays isn't anything that the children have yet experienced within the curriculum. We try to pinpoint things to make the children look, to make them want to learn, to make them go a bit further.'

- Provide opportunities for child-initiated learning and give children control of their own learning. Encourage thinking skills. (See below.)

- Lead to heightened achievement. (As one measure, Hackleton's SATs results have steadily improved since the beginning of this creative period, until they are now consistently rated among the top 50 primary schools in the country. A specific example is boys' writing, which four years before had been targeted as a problem. Boys found new enthusiasm in the curriculum flows. 'When for example the science came in to the history flow, the boys actually put pen to paper – they've been running round writing signs, making notes, writing instructions – things we didn't get from boys before.' Boys' writing is now above the national norm. Literacy results for both boys and girls are extremely healthy. Teachers attribute this to the meaningfulness and enjoyment of pupils' learning.)

Table 8.1 shows focus week six of the curriculum flow covered in Year 2, term 3. Previous weeks focused on: General overview of the Victorians; Victorian inventions; Our own great exhibition; What was it like for a poor child in the 1840s?; What would it have been like to go to the Victorian Hackleton? The final four weeks focus on: What was it like in the Crimea and how did Florence make it better for the soldiers?; Who was Mary Seacole and why did she go to the Crimea?; What was it like for Mary Seacole in the Crimea and how did she help?; What have we learnt about the Victorians, Florence and Mary?

Table 8.1 An example of part of a curriculum flow (illustrations not included)

Year 2 – Term 3 – Florence Nightingale and the Victorians (people who made a difference to other people's lives)

	Art	Science	History/geography	ICT	Music	Literacy	Numeracy
Learning objective	Design and make a vehicle to move the wounded soldiers from the battlefields to Mary Seacole on the shore.	Make a Florence Nightingale three-layer dress. Discuss hygiene.	• To identify people from the present and past who are famous. • To identify how people became famous. • To infer information from pictures of the past. • To recognise similarities and differences between what people wear today and what people wore a long time ago. • Know about the life of a famous person from the past and why she acted as she did. • To infer information from a written or visual account of a person's life. • To locate the site of a historical event on a map.	Geog – find Crimea on map.	• To control pitch. • To control the expressive elements, e.g. timbre, dynamics, tempo. • To listen carefully and develop aural memory.	Cakes with Emma and planting bulbs (from 'The Gardener')	Read and begin to write the vocabulary related to capacity. Measure and compare using litres and millilitres and know the relationship between them. Suggest suitable units, equipment to estimate or measure capacity. Read scales. Record measurements using mixed units or to the nearest whole/half unit (e.g. 3.5 litres).

Table 8.1 continued overleaf

Table 8.1 continued

	Art	Sci	History/geography	ICT	Music	Literacy	Numeracy
Activity/resources	Vehicles to move soldiers from the battlefields.		**Key Question** – Who was Florence Nightingale? PPt Florence 1 Florence 2 Links Think about what the word 'famous' means. Who do they know who is famous? Why is he or she famous? What other famous people from the past do they know about? What did they do to become famous? How do we find out about famous people? Tell the children that Florence was a famous person who lived a long time ago, before even their parents/carers and grandparents were alive. Thinking skills – use task wheel **Obj** – Make a list of questions that could be answered by looking at a picture. E.g. *What is she wearing? What is she doing? Does the picture show what is happening today or something that happened a long time ago?* Show children a picture of Florence Nightingale in nurse's uniform. (Use front of Big Book) Answer questions made by children – put facts into Florence Museum *What did they find out about her from this picture? Are the clothes like the clothes women wear now? How are they different? Can you think of any people today who wear the same sort of clothes? What do they do? What work might the person in the picture do? How can we tell that this person lived a very long time ago? What sort of person do you think she is?*	Find pencil/black and white portraits of Florence.	Where is love?	Why have the boxes been waiting for her? Why does Uncle Jim not smile? PHSE Write poem he pats. Draw picture she draws to Grandma. The secret space. Where is it? What is it? Design what to do with the space.	Continued sales from great exhibition.

	Art	Sci	History/geography	ICT	Music	Literacy	Numeracy
Activity/resources			Tell the children that Florence Nightingale lived in Victorian times and place her correctly on a timeline. Show pictures of Queen Victoria. Discuss did Florence and QV come before or after the Fire of London? http://www.bbc.co.uk/education/dynamo/history/stepback.htm **Key Question** – Why did Florence Nightingale go to the Crimea? Look at start up History Big Book – p.4 uses the word 'famous' as discussed in a previous session. Look at the picture of the hospital p.5 – what do they notice about it? List facts. Ask where or what is the Crimea? (pp.6–7) Why was Florence there? (pp.8–9) Introduce Sidney Herbert. (p.9)				
Assess	Vehicle must resemble something that could have been used during the Crimean war. Do children remember axle and chassis from previous vehicle work? Can they still construct them successfully?	Successfully make doll. Be able to say why it would be difficult to nurse in such a uniform. Would it be as hygienic as a modern nurse?	Identify present and past people who are famous, and explain why they are famous. Describe clothes worn a long time ago. Suggest what is different about Florence Nightingale's clothes from clothes worn by women of all generations today. Extract some information about the early life of Florence Nightingale from a video. Identify how Florence Nightingale travelled. Explain that journeys in the past used to take longer and were dangerous.	Easily use internet to find and use data to support curriculum work.	Begin to sing with control of pitch, e.g. following the shape of the melody. Make connections between symbols and sounds showing understanding of how sounds go higher and lower.		

At the end of term three, the class look back over the whole year, considering 'What have we learnt this year?' These are the guidelines:

Learning objectives

- Review each subject through whole topic approach.
- Can the children remember what art they did in Fire of London?
- Ditto in Egypt etc?
- Why do they think they remember the things they do? Were they practical activities for some children? Did others prefer books?

Activity/resources

- List activities for each subject.
- Children discuss preferences and present in a variety of ways things they liked and what helped them learn.
- Decide as a class one thing for each subject that they preferred most over the year.

Assess

- For children to realise 'how they learn best'.
- For them to know how to apply their best learning patterns to subjects in the future.
- To bring year to a full and constructive close.

Creative learning

We'll focus on one example that goes with the Florence Nightingale flow in Table 8.1 and that illustrates the experiential learning involved.

Class 2 are set a problem. Dawn first revises some key details about Florence Nightingale (the facts have been well learned by the children!). Florence is to receive 12 injured soldiers, but there are no beds in the hospital at Scutari. The children must help Florence find space in her ward for 12 beds and a heater. The beds must all be 10 cm long and 5 cm wide, and there must be a 1 cm space around the beds so their nurses can get between them. They must also make a log to decide how many bandages, blankets, nurses and meals they will need.

Dawn divides the time available into thinking time, plenary discussion, doing time, then final plenary. She prompts and motivates – 'Talk about it first, we want lots of ideas, don't just have one idea and think that's it. Think about possible problems and go back and see if you can think of something better.' She emphasises the importance of *sharing* ideas.

There is much animated talk in the groups in the thinking time, a veritable cauldron of ideas production. In the first plenary there is much discussion with the children volunteering points such as 'you can't put beds together or against a wall'. Dawn does not judge, there are no wrong ideas. They discuss cutting, drawing, where the beds might go.

For the doing, Dawn advises they allocate roles. Every child must be involved. Dawn has loads of resources, gives out paper, squared paper, stick-its, paste, glue, Blu-Tack, coloured paper. During the second plenary, the groups come together to examine each other's designs. They present their plans, explaining the ideas behind them, problems they had and how they solved them, and answer questions from the other groups.

After tidying up, there are a few minutes left, so Dawn plays a 20 questions-type game. This is a good example of teaching in the margins. She is somebody to do with Florence Nightingale and the class have to ask her factual questions to which she can only reply yes or no. This is a fun way of revising essential facts learned so far.

At the end of this session, Dawn says that so far they have been making 2D models. She wants them next time to make a 3D model. She wants them to put design into practice, turn the classroom into a hospital reality and act out their roles. This is how they make the skills and knowledge their own.

There has to be a sound basis of facts first, and Dawn had a creative way of teaching and learning them. They were not just learning these things for the sake of it. They have to apply what they know, and in doing so find out more. The children have to find out facts from the Internet, CD-ROMs and books. Class 6 children help them with the books through 'reading conferencing'. In the course of their research the children came across a number of references to Mary Seacole. Dawn encouraged them to find out more about her and compare her to Florence. The Class 2 children wrote facts on stick-its and put them on a chart in the centre of the table. They were asked to predict whether there were more similarities or differences between Florence and Mary, and then to sort the facts accordingly:

> It was only actually when they started to work out their own facts and then split them out in similarities and differences that they saw the amount of differences that they had in comparison to Florence Nightingale, which I thought was a bit of a shock really, and then to see not particularly how easy Florence Nightingale had it in her hospital with her Nightingale Nurses and in comparison to Mary Seacole who had her soldiers on the shore. I felt it was an invaluable learning opportunity for them really. It would have been easy for me to sit there with a book and show them and tell them those facts in far less time than they had to create 'Scutari' here in the classroom but I can guarantee now the fact that they have taken charge of their own learning and they have actually done that and there has been an emotional response they're not going to forget that for a long time now.

Having a sound basis in the facts and having done some preliminary designs, the children were then given the task of transforming their classroom into Scutari. First, in small groups in the ICT suite, they discussed measurements, spacing and arrangements round the computers, imagining how things would be. They then used and developed their ICT skills to draw floor plans of Florence's hospital based on the facts and pictures they had seen. When they returned to the classroom Dawn allocated jobs in closed envelopes. Some were to help Florence in Scutari, some Mary on the Black Sea coast. Each group had to arrange the beds in the space available to accommodate 12 soldiers, and find or make and have ready the requisite number of bandages, blankets, nurses and meals, so many per soldier. These details were put on a log and pinned to the board. Everybody had to be involved and all had to have a role in the completed ward. The task had to be done in a certain time and Dawn would remind them at regular intervals. There was a clear objective but the children were given no structural or procedural guidance. Dawn wanted to see 'what they came up with'. A wide range of resources was ready for them to use.

When told they could start, the classroom became a feverish maelstrom of noise and activity, with the teacher standing back surveying the scene. Children were thinking, discussing, reviewing resources, cutting or tearing cloth, laying coloured paper on the floor, pasting, glueing, moving furniture, fetching utensils, going in and out of the room taking some stuff out and other stuff in. Somebody divided the room into two, and gradually out of the chaos, order began to emerge, desks taking the place of beds in Florence's ward, with covers, drinks, plates for meals, and eventually wounded soldiers suitably bandaged lying on the beds attended by Florence and her nurses, all acting out their roles. In Mary's half, as it was a beach, the beds were blankets on the ground. And in one corner the bookshelves had been converted into Mary's shop, stocked with all the things she used to sell, such as boots (trainers from PE kits!).

Dawn comments on the variety of learning opportunities:

It's a shame really that you don't have 26 pairs of eyes to see all the things that are happening but I did notice in the Scutari Hospital that a child had put a chair in the centre of the room and the chair became redder and redder with the amount of material that was being put on it. And when I asked her about this she said 'when we were doing our research we noticed there was a heater in the centre of the room in the Scutari Hospital'. And then I looked over here and all of a sudden children were taking musical instruments off shelves and going outside and getting their trainers. You don't need to be scared when they start dismantling your classroom and then disappearing out of the door! That's fine, we do need a hospital here, but why are you going to get your trainers? Because it says in the book that Mary Seacole sold boots. Fantastic! And then I noticed whole heaps of chairs going out of the door and when I asked the children 'well plastic wasn't invented then'. And there are all of these things. A child had the idea of laying a line in the centre of the room to split Scutari Hospital up from the shore, but they decided that wasn't good enough. It needed to look like water so they covered the line with blue pieces of paper that they found in the sorting boxes. Then another child said 'but it still really doesn't look like the shore, we need to cover the shore with sand', so he got some more yellow pieces of paper and he actually covered the shore and by doing these things it actually gave an insight in to how hard it was for Mary Seacole to do her nursing. Not only did they have to get round their beds, but they had to trample over this tissue paper, which actually would have been how hard it was to walk around the soldiers. And those are the types of opportunities that come out and you'd never thought of them yourself.

Doing it for real like this enables the children to experience the problems and appreciate the feelings. It draws them closer to knowledge, helps them internalise it, make it their own, and remember it.

Dawn acted as facilitator and consolidator asking questions at key points. Generally she used open-ended questions – 'So what else?' 'How could you?' 'How would you?' 'What would Mary have done?' Sometimes more specific prompts were needed. With 20 minutes left, the Mary Seacole side seemed to Dawn not to have enough beds. Such was the pressure on space; they seemed not to have noticed. So Dawn called a time check, and took the opportunity to raise the point. 'We only have 20 minutes left now and you're soon going to receive your 12 soldiers. Do you have your beds for them?' They actually had problems in the general chaos in seeing how many beds they had, until one girl suggested they could number the beds. Doing this revealed that they were three short. But they had not enough space left. This led to more group discussion on how the plan could be adjusted to accommodate the further three beds, which they eventually accomplished, though it was a tight squeeze – not unlike the reality. Dawn commented: 'It would have been easy for me to stop them and tell them they hadn't enough beds, but if they can realise it themselves then they have ownership of their own learning and they feel it's them that were successful, not because I told them.'

In the debriefing, Dawn reinforced facts and emotional connections by asking judicious questions: 'What would it be like to be a nurse?' 'What would be one of the hardest things?' 'Is it easy to get round those beds?' 'How does it compare with nursing today?' 'What's it like lying on those beds?'

Dawn says their curriculum is 'an ongoing process and not set in stone. You are always coming across new materials and ideas, lots of them from the children.'

Conclusion

There are contrary forces at work and contrary experiences going on in primary schools, but at least some schools, like Hackleton (there are others – see, for example, the QCA website http://curriculum.qca.org.uk), are finding more space and opportunities to put into practice their own brand of teaching around what they see as the undisputed strengths of the National Curriculum.

Moreover, their enterprise has received high plaudits from Ofsted. The full inspection of November 2004 showed the school to be 'at the cutting edge of curriculum development and gives pupils a wonderful introduction to lifelong learning'. Teachers were praised for their 'vision, innovation and a complete lack of complacency'. There was a 'vibrant and innovative curriculum' and there were 'excellent opportunities for pupils to take charge of their own learning and to show initiative'. There was 'a vibrant and busy atmosphere in a school awash with outstanding displays that celebrate pupils' work and excite interest'. Through 'excellent initiatives, the learning environment is so attractive that pupils are eager to come to school'. Their 'enjoyment of school is written on their faces and reflected in their good attendance'. 'Ingenious schemes have been put in place.' The school is a 'warm, welcoming and uplifting environment where smiles abound and each day offers exciting learning opportunities'. The inspectors had no criticisms at all to make of Hackleton. This is a ringing endorsement of the creative teaching practices under development here, and an encouragement to other schools.

The school subsequently was named as a 'Particularly Successful School' in the Chief HMI's report; and also received a Leading School Award for 'Inspirational Teaching, Excellence and Enjoyment through an Innovative Curriculum'. Hackleton was also chosen as a Research School by the National College of School Leaders (NCSL). Other accolades have followed. The school was given the 'Leading Aspect Award' certificate and plaque for motivating children with its curriculum and creating a 'positive learning zone'. Hackleton was invited by the QCA to take part in a video on creativity they were making for the benefit of all primary schools (QCA 2005). Some of the film not used by the QCA was requested by Creative Partnerships for use in a training project for Advanced Skills Teachers across the country.

Recently, the school changed its status to a Church of England (VA) school and necessarily was required to have another inspection, which came at very short notice. The Inspectors' report in January 2007 was even more glowing than the previous one, the school being judged as 'outstanding' in 25 out of 26 categories. The following selected comments show how Hackleton's development of creative learning has succeeded, and how it meets with official approval:

Pupils care for each other, valuing each other's opinions. Pupils' personal development and well-being are outstanding. Pupils love school and there is a buzz of excitement as they eagerly carry out their work. One pupil said 'I love learning', and another 'I can't wait to build the pyramid as part of our work about Egypt'. Pupils are very confident and greatly enjoy responsibility and having a say in how the school is run.

The youngest children enjoy a range of exciting activities within a caring and sensitive environment. This provides a springboard for their love of learning; they make good progress and attain standards above those expected.

Stimulating activities are at the heart of outstanding teaching and learning. Teachers are imaginative in finding ways to involve pupils in learning and to widen their horizons through an exciting range of experiences. The outstanding curriculum is fun, creative and stimulating. It is complemented very well by a rich diet of additional activities including visits, visitors and after school clubs.

Pupils are urged to do their best, but there is also a strong sense of fun and enjoyment in lessons that keep all pupils motivated. They are encouraged to take the initiative and teachers very effectively build on these skills so that the pupils are able to work and learn independently. For example, pupils learn how to judge the quality of others' work so that they can more critically examine their own.

(Ofsted 2007, pp. 2–4)

Creative thinking is currently being encouraged outside the conventional curriculum at Hackleton, notably through the School Council, which is managed and run by the children. Here they are encouraged to adopt creative approaches but in a democratic and ethical way. The children have set up a snack shack for healthy snacks, initiated playground/environmental projects, liaised with the local community over end-of-school parking issues, and made reports to the governing body. Creativity is not just for lessons – it's for citizenship.

The SATs hold no fears for most of Hackleton's children, perhaps because they achieve so highly. 'When we had our assessment week, Charlie came in and said, "this is my favourite week" … On the whole, they quite like them, strange children!' The staff, though, are no supporters of performativity. They prefer their own assessment system, where

the class teachers aren't filling out a ridiculous amount of tick boxes about their children. The assessment is very meaningful, it's based on clear objectives and class teachers know precisely when, at the end of each unit in what subject, and the details all feed through to my laptop 'cos we've got the net working now and it's good and it's meaningful, and it does help children and it does move them on. The problem with SATs is that to throw those papers to children that have nothing to do with anything we think they're doing anyway – when their whole lives are being enriched, with everything being meaningful to them, linking their learning, and they can use their knowledge, and wham! you put this thing in front of them ... the government need to look at that.

(Dawn, HT)

The structures of performativity are still very much in place – the government controls, the bureaucratic procedures. Creative teachers are trying to break free of these shackles. It is not accomplished overnight or even in a year. Hackleton has shown how a start can be made which almost generates its own impetus, given the leadership, dedication, conviction and resolve among its staff. Other schools can at least take heart from such developments. They can structure their curricula, organise their classrooms and their teaching, rediscover their vocational commitment, enjoy their work, help students to higher and higher levels of learning, in ways that have not been possible for many teachers since the early 1980s. But can this be maintained?

9   The future of creative learning

There are a number of favourable conditions for achieving innovation. On the basis of our researches, a form of democratic participation would appear to be the management structure most conducive to pupil empowerment (Carrington and Short 1989; Trafford 1993). Social constructivism, with its emphasis on pupil ownership of knowledge and control of learning processes and social context, seems the most favourable learning theory (Pollard 1991); though it needs to be 'strong' rather than 'weak' constructivism (Watts and Bentley 1991). The latter might suffer the fate of Plowdenism and become transformed into an ideology (Alexander 1992). Pupil involvement in control of their learning (Oldroyd and Tiller 1987; Rowland 1987) and in the evaluation of their work (Armstrong 1992; Towler and Broadfoot 1992; Quicke and Winter 1993) is necessary. In general, pupil 'voices' need to be heard (Fielding 2007). As Qvortrup (1990, p. 94) argues, 'If we seriously mean to improve life conditions for children we must, as a minimum precondition, establish reporting systems in which they are heard themselves as well as reported on by others' (see also Paley 1986). We also need a curriculum where the central aim is the 'promotion of the student's well-being as a self-determining citizen ...' (O'Hear and White 1991, p. 6). Above all, perhaps, there can be no innovative students without creative teachers, which, as we have noted, intensification and the culture of performativity does not encourage.

However, we do not lack this particular resource and it has survived the stultifying central pressures of the 1990s. We have noted (Woods 1995) how some teachers when under pressure engage in 'resistance' and 'appropriation'; how 'cultures of collaboration' (Nias *et al.* 1989) can develop, and self-determination become generated; how potentially alienative forces can be 'recognised', and how teachers' own philosophies and goals can be more clearly 'identified'; how potentially alienative changes can be 'engaged with', and 'alliances' formed. Such teachers and schools have managed to integrate the subject-based National Curriculum around their own distinctive relational ideas (Bernstein 1975; Maw 1993); and generated a form of power that is positive and productive in the realisation of their aims (Foucault 1980).

The most important factor, perhaps, is an officially sanctioned creativity discourse, and we have seen in this book how some schools and teachers seem to be thriving on this. Hackleton's experience in Chapter 8, for example, seems a happy story from the creative point of view. However, it has to be said that many schools are still finding it difficult to cope with the performativist pressures. Galton and MacBeath (2002), for example, found a very different situation in the schools of their research. In those schools, at the very point where Hackleton was beginning to break free,

- art and music were being squeezed out;
- the curriculum had been narrowed;
- teachers spent a day a week on testing;
- large numbers of 5–7-year-olds were tested each week;
- the decline in creative subjects was matched by a decline in teachers' own sense of creativity;
- whole-class teaching had more than doubled since 1976;
- teachers' hours were up 10 per week since 1971;
- a DfES spokeswoman commented: 'we will not apologise for raising standards and we are not about to change a strategy admired around the world. Children cannot learn anything until they get the basics right.'

Perhaps, though, creativity and performativity are not total opposites? A measure of prescription might remain in the National Curriculum, as every child's basic right; on the whole, teachers agree with what is there, and there have undoubtedly been benefits, such as the advances in the teaching of certain subjects like science. Schools like Hackleton have now found room to cover it within their own curriculum in their own 'creative' way (for another example, see Jeffrey and Woods 2003). We have also seen in Chapter 6 how creative teachers used certain aspects of the new legislation to enhance their creativity, such as clarifying their intentions, reconstructing a relevant pedagogy, and developing a language for learners that would assist their control and ownership. With such careful planning of intentions, processes and evaluation, the mistakes of the child-centred teaching of the 1970s in the wake of the Plowden report, so starkly revealed by Alexander (1992), and so savaged in the government rhetoric and policies of the day, might be avoided. Chapter 7 is another case study of how schools are using external agencies to prise open the spaces on offer from the way the creativity discourse has influenced government policy but these are tentative steps due to the influence of the standards agenda which still dominates policy.

There is a distinct move, too, in Ofsted literature toward an integrated curriculum, while keeping faith with subjects; and originality, imagination and interest are stressed. The 2003 *Handbook for Inspection* stated that, for a school meriting the highest rating:

Imaginative curriculum design promotes high achievement. Subjects or areas of learning are interlinked, without losing their discrete nature, to provide a range of connected experiences ... carefully managed innovations help to meet changing requirements. All classrooms and other areas for learning (including outdoors) are organised imaginatively and resourced to provide interesting experiences.

(Ofsted 2003b, p. 79)

We saw these principles put into effect in Chapter 8 at Hackleton. On the basis of the two inspections at that school, there would appear, too, to be less stark differences in cultural values between inspectors and teachers, the former now recognising and applauding the collegiality, professionalism and self-regulation of the latter, in contrast to some Ofsted inspections of the 1990s (see Jeffrey and Woods 1998). This may, of course, not reflect all primary schools' experience or all Ofsted teams.

Perhaps creativity and performativity *are* essentially competing discourses. However, in practice one is never without the other. There always has been, even in Plowden days, a large measure of transmission teaching in primary schools, and some creativity survived the constraints of the 1990s. Now that Woodhead's (1995) recommended 60 per cent of whole-class teaching has faded into history, these values are less polarised, and teachers can avail themselves of whatever methods suit their purposes. We saw in Chapter 6 how some teachers, in response to the reforms, re-fashioned their use of direct teaching to the benefit of their creative teaching; equally, in Chapter 8, we saw how Ofsted were highly supportive of the whole range of creative methods being used at Hackleton.

There are certainly still big differences between the discourses, notably in assessment. The government continues to take a stubborn stance with regard to what the vast majority of teachers regard as the anti-educational SATs, though some modifications have been made, and the Welsh Assembly has abolished them in their schools. The government can make all the noises it wishes about championing creativity, but changing the performative structures is seen as a political non-starter. Within the performativity discourse, how is creative teaching to be evaluated? How is it conceived? What is it for?

Creative learning has a number of consequences for individuals, learner identities and self-hood, pedagogy, life-long learning and school and government policies. It is clear from our research that creative teaching and learning is a holistic approach that engages the learner's experience, imagination, emotions and sociability. It is inclusive, encourages negotiation with teachers and peers, engages learners in democratic practices, celebrates achievement and originality and models appreciation of others. It is investigative, enquiry led, challenging, encourages possibility thinking and prioritises process over product. It lays the basis for interest in a life-wide creativity, for an experience of the joy of learning, for co-participation, collective endeavour, collaboration and teamwork. The evidence presented in this book suggests that creativity teaching and learning may become institutionalised within the curriculum and pedagogies of schools due to the strong reappearance of a creativity discourse, the practical outcomes of which have been welcomed by Ofsted, as we saw in Chapter 8. We also showed earlier that this discourse exists alongside a set of powerful performativity policies which sometimes restrict and constrain creativity policies and schools. Teachers are currently managing the tension between the two. It is as yet unclear as to how this situation may change for as this book goes to press there are examples of this tension being played out at government level. The recent Government Select Committee Report into testing and assessment (House of Commons Children, Schools and Families Committee 2008) has highlighted the assertion that English students are one of the most highly tested groups in Europe. It recommends a reduction in standardised testing which is seen as mainly for school accountability and used to rank schools for performance. The report recommends more reliance on formative assessment for all-round learner improvement. The report's conclusions are supported by the results from the most extensive research project into the state of primary schools in England since the 1960s (Alexander 2008), which also condemns the effects of testing on the primary school curriculum and pedagogies and recommends a broader approach to assessment focusing on more summative assessments and wider accountability criteria than tests. Notwithstanding the weight of these arguments and evidence, the government has declared its firm support for the continuation of its testing policies, in the interests of more demonstrable improvement along a more narrow front, albeit with recommendations for more flexible time schedules for testing, leading to testing when students are ready to progress.

Added to these specific tensions is a new reform programme for primary schools scheduled to come into effect in 2010. This will update the educational reforms of the early 1990s along the same lines. Thus, there will be the embedding of more frequent, but less intensive, Ofsted inspections, a new curriculum, an extension of testing and assessment, and an integration of children's services and education. It is, as yet, unclear as to what extent creative teaching and learning will be supported in these new arrangements. On the one hand there has been nominal support from government as indicated in the main introduction and the practice is being taken up by a number of schools. But the performative structures and discourse remain in place.

According to the Cambridge research project, the dominant development in primary schools is not creative learning as such, but the management of emotions to 'overcome (self-imposed) barriers to the achievement of learning goals'. Their examination of alternative schools, which the report finds are as successful as state schools, shows that they share the following in common:

- Significantly less time spent using televisions and computers;
- Significantly more time spent on reading with and to children;

- Greater emphasis on the life use of the imagination;
- Closer relationships between student and teacher.

The report suggests that the influence of educational alternatives and private initiatives may increase, and that we must pay attention to the emotions and dispositions – behavioural attitudes to learning in the educational process.

The main point to note from this report is the assertion that policies on curriculum and pedagogy are open to external influence and presumably we could add the educational creative learning discourse. Nevertheless, the report also shows many other influences, for example learning to learn, assessment for learning, activating children's thinking skills, cognitive acceleration through science, maths and technical education, and thinking through geography (Conroy *et al.* 2008).

Creative learning policies are not obviously in abundance, but there are some promising developments as discussed in this book. Also, there is one significant alliance that could increase the influence of those supporting creative learning. Young participants' voices in teaching and learning are increasingly prominent. The UN Rights of the Child and the 'Every Child Matters' policy legislate for the inclusion of pupil voice in decisions taken about their education (James *et al.* 1997; Lewis and Lindsay 2000). The Teaching and Learning Research Programme has produced research to show how teaching and learning could be improved with the engagement of pupil voice (Rudduck and Flutter 2000; Rudduck *et al.* 2004; Rudduck and McIntyre 2007). There are pupil voice toolkits on the QCA website, and citizenship policies and programmes devote a significant amount of time to its inclusion (MacBeath *et al.* 2003). Further, the government has published a 'Children's Plan' to focus on their needs. Primary learners' voices are promoted by the establishment of student councils in many schools including one in our study, and the quality of their perspectives has been exemplified many times (Jeffrey 2001a, 2001b, 2005; Pollard *et al.* 2000). These developments are also linked to the promotion of the democratisation of schooling (Fielding 2007). However, the support for pupil voice is problematic and there are also warnings about the danger that the process of pupil consultation is one which hides power relations (ibid.). Nevertheless, the development of a participative enquiry between young participants and teachers and between peers, teaching and learning strategies with young participants and the inclusion of pupil voice in how to improve the quality of teaching and learning are major movements in education and an indisputable boost to creative learning.

A second favourable influence is in the area of teacher commitment. We have found in other studies that teacher well-being and commitment is influenced by the extent to which they themselves are able to be creative and to provide creative learning for their young participants (Troman *et al.* 2007). Recent policies are focusing on teacher well-being and professional satisfaction, challenging the intensification of work that has reduced their effectiveness (Jeffrey and Woods 1997; Osborn *et al.* 2000).

A third influence is with what appears to be a continually evolving curriculum with the latest reinterpretation being the Primary National Strategy published in 2004 as an example. Yet another development is projected for 2010. The QCA, who will be making a major contribution to this independent review through inviting perspectives from across education, has asked the authors of it to:

- be concerned with the development of the whole child and not just their level of attainment;
- consider whether all subjects need to start in Year 1;
- consider whether aspects of the foundation stage should be extended into the primary curriculum (QCA 2007a).

The first request reflects one of the characteristics of creative learning, that of engaging with the whole child, and one of the main aspects of the foundation curriculum is that of promoting creativity. The QCA (2007b, pp. 262–263) suggests that holistic learning which

> [provides] an inspiring and challenging curriculum that is concerned with 'the whole child' is a challenge. Schools are trying to deliver the National Curriculum, while adding their own unique emphases to achieve both excellence and enjoyment. Some are adapting programmes of study to suit children and local needs, for example, and giving children wider experiences to help them develop their personal skills and creativity.

They go on to ask contributors to send in their views on the importance of the following which they think will achieve the current Minister of State's aim to promote lifelong learning:

- Enjoying learning. It seems unlikely that anyone who disliked learning at school would be keen to continue doing it all their lives.
- Achieving some success in learning. People who experience success in learning are more likely to continue than those who have always failed. This does not mean 'dumbing down' so that everyone can succeed. It means building further learning on what is already known and understood, and designing compelling learning experiences that are personalised to different needs.
- Seeing the point of learning. When learning is relevant to people's lives and circumstances, and they can see the benefits, they are more likely to want to continue (QCA 2007c).

The first and last points appear to reflect our 'relevance' aspect of creative learning, the second, our 'ownership' of learning. There are clearly current opportunities for creative learning to become a major factor in teaching and learning in primary schools for many years to come, but those with an interest in it will need to take every opportunity to influence the policy texts (Ball 1994) that abound to ensure its place in a future primary education system.

References

Alexander, R. (1992) *Policy and Practice in Education.* London: Routledge.

Alexander, R. (2004) Still no pedagogy? Principle, pragmatism and compliance in primary education. *Cambridge Journal of Education* 34(1), pp. 7–33.

Alexander, R. (2008) *The Primary Review: The Condition and Future of Primary Education in England.* Cambridge: Cambridge University.

Alexander, R., Rose, J. and Woodhead, C. (1992) *Curriculum Organisation and Classroom Practice in Primary Schools: A Discussion Paper.* London: HMSO.

Anderson, G.L. (1989) Critical ethnography in education: origins, current status and new directions. *Review of Educational Research* 59(3), pp. 249–270.

Apple, M. (1986) *Teachers and Texts.* London: Routledge and Kegan Paul.

Armstrong, M. (1992) Rendering an account. In Burgess, T. (ed.) *Accountability in Schools.* London: Longman.

Ball, S.J. (ed.) (1990) *Foucault and Education: Disciplines and Knowledge.* London: Routledge.

Ball, S.J. (1994) *Education Reform: A Critical and Post-structural Approach.* Buckingham: Open University Press.

Ball, S.J. (1997) Good School/Bad School: paradox and fabrication. *British Journal of Sociology in Education* 18(3), pp. 317–337.

Ball, S.J. (1998) Performativity and fragmentation in 'Postmodern Schooling'. In Carter, J. (ed.) *Postmodernity and Fragmentation of Welfare.* London: Routledge, pp. 187–203.

Ball, S.J. (2000) Performativities and fabrications in the education economy: towards the performative society? *Australian Educational Researcher* 27(2), pp. 1–23.

Ball, S.J. (2003) The teacher's soul and the terrors of performativity. *Journal of Education Policy* 18(2), pp. 215–228.

Ball, S.J. and Bowe, R. (1992) Subject departments and the 'implementation' of National Curriculum Policy: an overview of the issues. *Journal of Curriculum Studies* 24(2), pp. 97–115.

Beetlestone, F. (1998) *Creative Children, Imaginative Teaching.* Buckingham: Open University Press.

Berger, P.L. and Luckmann, T. (1976) *Sociology: A Biographical Approach.* London: Penguin.

Bernstein, B. (1971) On the classification and framing of educational knowledge. In Young, M.F.D. (ed.) *Knowledge and Control: New Directions for the Sociology of Education.* London: Collier Macmillan, pp. 47–69.

Bernstein, B. (1975) *Class, Codes and Control, Vol. 3: Towards a Theory of Educational Transmissions.* London: Routledge and Kegan Paul.

Best, P., Craft, A. and Jeffrey, B. (2004) Creative friends model within creative partnerships. *Black Country Evaluation Report.* Black Country Creative Partnerships.

Black, P., Swann, J. and Dylan, W. (2006) School pupils' beliefs about learning. *Research Papers in Education* 21(2), pp. 151–170.

Boostrom, R. (1994) Learning to pay attention. *Qualitative Studies in Education* 7(1), pp. 51–64.

Breakwell, G.M. (1986) *Coping with Threatened Identities.* London: Methuen.

Brehony, K. (1992) What's left of progressive education? In Rattansi, A. and Reeder, D. (eds) *Rethinking Radical Education: Essays in Honour of Brian Simon.* London: Lawrence and Wishart.

Bridges, D. (1991) From teaching to learning. *The Curriculum Journal* 2(2), pp. 137–151.

Bruner, J. (1986) *Actual Minds, Possible Worlds.* London: Harvard University Press.

Bruner, J.S. (1972) *The Relevance of Education.* Harmondsworth: Penguin.

Campbell, R.J. (1993a) The National Curriculum in primary schools: a dream at conception, a nightmare at delivery. In Chitty, C. and Simon, B. (eds) *Education Answers Back: Critical Responses to Government Policy.* London: Lawrence and Wishart.

Campbell, R.J. (1993b) The broad and balanced curriculum in primary schools: some limitations on reform. *The Curriculum Journal* 4(2), pp. 215–229.

Camsey, S. (1989) Evaluation of E-Mail Project, Barnehurst Junior School, Kent.

Carrington, B. and Short, G. (1989) *'Race' and the Primary School.* Slough: NFER-Nelson.

Claxton, G. (1999) *Wise Up: The Challenge of Life Long Learning.* London: Bloomsbury.

Claydon, E., Desforges, C., Mills, C. and Rawson, W. (1994) Authentic activity and learning. *British Journal of Educational Studies* 42(2), pp. 163–173.

Cocklin, B., Coombe, K. and Retallick, J. (1999) Learning communities in education: directions for professional development. In Cocklin, B., Coombe, K. and Retallick, J. (eds) *Learning Communities in Education.* London: Routledge.

Conroy, J., Hulme, M. and Menter, I. (2008) Primary curriculum cultures. In Alexander, S.R. (ed.) *The Primary Review.* Cambridge: University of Cambridge

Craft, A. (2002) *Creativity and Early Years Education.* London: Continuum.

Craft, A. (2003) The limits to creativity in education: dilemmas for the educator. *British Journal of Educational Studies* 51(2), pp. 113–127.

Craft, A. (2005) *Creativity in Schools: Tensions and Dilemmas.* London: Routledge.

Craft, A. and Jeffrey, B. (2004) Learner inclusiveness for creative learning. *Education 3–13* 32(2), pp. 39–43.

Croll, P. (1996) *Teachers, Pupils and Primary Schooling: Continuity and Change.* London: Cassell.

Dadds, M. (1994) The changing face of topic work in the primary curriculum. *The Curriculum Journal* 4(2), pp. 253–266.

Dadds, M. (2001) The politics of pedagogy. *Teachers and Teaching* 7(1), pp. 43–58

Davies, L. (1999) Researching democratic understanding in primary school. *Research in Education* 61(May), pp. 39–48.

Dewey, J. (1929) *The Quest for Certainty: A Study of the Relation of Knowledge and Action*. New York: Minton, Balch.

DfES (2003a) *Excellence and Enjoyment: A Strategy for Primary Schools*. London: DfES.

DfES (2003b) *Report of the Joint DfES/DCMS Creativity Seminar for LEAs*. London: DfES.

Donnington, C., Flutter, J. and Rudduck, J. (2000) Taking their word for it: can listening and responding to pupils' views give new directions to school improvement? *Education 3–13* 28(3), pp. 46–51.

Dowrick, N. (1993) Side by side: a more appropriate form of peer interaction for infant pupils. *British Educational Research Journal* 19(5), 499–515.

Duffield, J., Allen, J. and Turner, E. (2000) Pupils' voices on achievement: an alternative to the standards agenda. *Cambridge Journal of Education* 30(2), pp. 263–274.

Edwards, D. and Mercer, N. (1987) *Common Knowledge: The Development of Understanding in Classrooms*. London: Methuen.

Elbaz, F. (1992) Hope, attentiveness, and caring for difference: the moral voice in teaching. *Teaching and Teacher Education* 8(5/6), pp. 411–432.

Emilia, M.R. (1996) *The Hundred Languages of Children*. Reggio Emilia: Reggio Children.

Fielding, M. (2007) Beyond 'voice': new roles, relations, and contexts in researching with young people. *Discourse* 3(3), pp. 301–310.

Fletcher, C., Caron, M. and Williams, W. (1985) *Schools on Trial: The Trials of Democratic Comprehensives*. Milton Keynes: Open University Press.

Foucault, M. (ed.) (1980) *Power/Knowledge: Selected Interviews and Other Writings*. New York: Pantheon.

Fox, C. (1989) Children thinking through story. *English in Education* 23(2), pp. 33–42.

Freire, P. (1972) *Pedagogy of the Oppressed*. New York: Seabury.

Galton, M. and MacBeath, J. (2002) *Primary Teaching 1970–2000*. Report commissioned by the NUT. London: NUT.

Haigh, G. (1987) Pace-makers. *The Times Educational Supplement*, 18 December.

Halliwell, S. (1993) Teacher creativity and teacher education. In Bridges, D. and Kerry, T. (eds) *Developing Teachers Professionally*. London: Routledge.

Hargreaves, A. (1988) Teaching quality: a sociological analysis. *Journal of Curriculum Studies* 20(3), pp. 211–231.

Hargreaves, A. (1994) *Changing Teachers, Changing Times – Teachers' Work and Culture in the Postmodern Age*. London: Cassell.

Hartley, D. (2003) The instrumentalisation of the expressive in education. *British Journal of Educational Studies* 51(1), pp. 6–19.

Herzberg, F. (1971) Motivation-hygiene theory. In Pugh, D. (ed.) *Organisation Theory*. Harmondsworth: Penguin.

Hitchcock, G. and Hughes, D. (1995) *Research and the Teacher: A Qualitative Introduction to School-based Research*. London: Routledge.

House of Commons Children, Schools and Families Committee (2008) *Testing and Assessment: Government and Ofsted Response to Committee's Third Report of Session 2007–2008*. London: The Stationery Office.

Jackson, P.W. (1992) *Untaught Lessons*. New York: Teachers College Press.

James, A., Jenks, C. and Prout, A. (1997) *Theorising Childhood*. Cambridge: Polity Press.

Jeffrey, B. (2001a) Primary pupils' perspectives and creative learning. *Encyclopaideia (Italian Journal)* 9(Spring), 133–152.

Jeffrey, B. (2001b) Challenging prescription in ideology and practice: the case of Sunny First School. In Collins, J., Insley, K. and Soler, J. (eds) *Understanding Pedagogy*. Buckingham: Open University Press, pp. 143–160.

Jeffrey, B. (2002) Performativity and primary teacher relations. *Journal of Education Policy* 17(5), pp. 531–546.

Jeffrey, B. (2003) Countering student instrumentalism: a creative response. *British Educational Research Journal* 29(4), pp. 489–504.

Jeffrey, B. (2004) *Meaningful Creative Learning: Student Perspectives*. Crete: ECER.

Jeffrey, B. (2005) Creative learning and student perspectives. Swindon: CLASP ESRC.

Jeffrey, B. and Craft, A. (2001) The universalisation of creativity. In Craft, A., Jeffrey, B. and Leibling, M. (eds) *Creativity in Education*. London: Continuum, pp. 17–34.

Jeffrey, B. and Craft, A. (2004) Teaching creatively and teaching for creativity: distinctions and relationships. *Educational Studies* 30(1), pp. 77–87.

Jeffrey, B. and Woods, P. (1997) The relevance of creative teaching: pupils' views. In Pollard, A., Thiessen, D. and Filer, A. (eds) *Children and their Curriculum: The Perspectives of Primary and Elementary School Children*. London: Routledge/Falmer, pp. 15–33.

Jeffrey, B. and Woods, P. (1998) *Testing Teachers: The Effects of School Inspections on Primary Teachers*. London: Falmer.

Jeffrey, B. and Woods, P. (2003) *The Creative School: A Framework for Success, Quality and Effectiveness*. London: Routledge/Falmer.

Kane, R.G. and Maw, N. (2005) Making sense of learning at secondary school: involving students to improve teaching practice. *Cambridge Journal of Education* 35(3), pp. 311–322.

Lee, V. and Lee, J. (1987) Stories children tell. In Pollard, A. (ed.) *Children and Their Primary Schools*. Lewes: The Falmer Press.

Lewis, A. and Lindsay, G. (2000) *Researching Children's Perspectives*. Buckingham: Open University Press.

Lord, P. and Jones, M. (2006) *Pupils' Experiences and Perspectives of the National Curriculum: Research Review*. London: Qualifications and Curriculum Authority.

MacBeath, J. (2006) Finding a voice. *Educational Review* 58(2), pp. 195–207.

MacBeath, J., Demetriou, H., Rudduck, J. and Myers, K. (2003) *Consulting Pupils: A Toolkit for Teachers*. Cambridge: Pearson.

MacDonald, B. (1975) Evaluation and the control of education. In Tawney, D. (ed.) *Evaluation: The State of the Art*. London: Macmillan.

Maw, J. (1993) The National Curriculum Council and the whole curriculum: reconstruction of a discourse? *Curriculum Studies* 1(1), pp. 55–74.

Mead, G.H. (1934) *Mind, Self and Society*. Chicago: University of Chicago Press.

Measor, L. and Woods, P. (1984) *Changing Schools: Pupils' Perspectives on Transfer to a Comprehensive*. Milton Keynes: Open University Press.

Morris, E. (2001) *Professionalism and Trust – The Future of Teachers and Teaching*. Speech to the Social Market Foundation, November. London: DfEE.

Morrison, K. (1989) Bringing progressivism into a critical theory of education. *British Journal of Sociology of Education* 10(1), pp. 3–18.

NACCCE (1999) *All our Futures: Creativity, Culture and Education*. London: DfEE.

Nias, J. (1989) *Primary Teachers Talking*. London: Routledge.

Nias, J., Southworth, G. and Yeomans, R. (1989) *Staff Relationships in the Primary School: A Study of Organizational Cultures*. London: Cassell.

Noddings, N. (1992) *The Challenge to Care in Schools*. New York: Teachers College Press.

Ofsted (2001) *Improving Inspection, Improving Schools*. London: The Office for Standards in Education.

Ofsted (2003a) *Expecting the Unexpected: Developing Creativity in Primary and Secondary Schools*. London: Ofsted.

Ofsted (2003b) *Handbook for Inspecting Nursery and Primary Schools*. London: Ofsted.

Ofsted (2006) *Creative Partnerships: Initiative and Impact*. London: Ofsted.

Ofsted (2007) *Hackleton CofE Primary School Inspection Report*. London: Ofsted. Available at www.ofsted.gov.uk.

O'Hear, P. and White, J. (1991) *A National Curriculum for All: Laying the Foundations for Success*. London: Institute for Public Policy Research.

Oldroyd, D. and Tiller, T. (1987) Change from within: an account of school-based collaborative action research in an English secondary school. *Journal of Education for Teaching* 12(3), pp. 13–27.

Osborn, M. (1996) Teachers mediating change: Key Stage 1 revisited. In P. Croll (ed.) *Teachers, Pupils and Primary Schooling*. London: Cassell.

Osborn, M., McNess, E. and Broadfoot, P. (2000) *What Teachers Do: Changing Policy and Practice in Primary Education*. London: Continuum.

Paley, V.G. (1986) On listening to what the children say. *Harvard Educational Review* 26(2), pp. 122–131.

Pennuel, W.R. and Wertsch, J.V. (1995) Vygotsky and identity formation: a social cultural approach. *Educational Psychologist* 30(2), pp. 83–92.

Piaget, J. (1973) *The Child's Conception of the World*. St. Albans: Granada.

Plowden Report (1967) *Children and their Primary Schools*. Report of the Central Advisory Council for Education in England. London: HMSO.

Pollard, A. (1987) *Children and their Primary Schools*. Lewes: Falmer Press.

Pollard, A. (1990) Towards a sociology of learning in primary schools. *British Journal of Sociology of Education* 11(3), pp. 241–256.

Pollard, A. (1991) *Learning in Primary Schools*. London: Cassell.

Pollard, A. and Filer, A. (1999) *The Social World of Pupil Career*. London: Cassell.

Pollard, A., Broadfoot, P., Croll, P., Osborn, M. and Abbott, D. (1994) *Changing English Primary Schools? The Impact of the Education Reform Act at Key Stage One*. London: Cassell.

Pollard, A., Triggs, E. and Broadfoot, P. (2000) *What Pupils Say: Changing Policy and Practice in Primary Education*. London: Continuum.

QCA (1999) *Assessment and Reporting Arrangements*. London: DfEE.

QCA (2003) *Creativity: Find it, Promote it*. London: QCA.

QCA (2005) *Creativity Across the Curriculum*. Video. London: QCA.

QCA (2007a) *A Remit for Change*. Available at http://www.qca.org.uk/qca_15944.aspx (last updated March 2008).

QCA (2007b) *Focusing on the Whole Child*. Available at http://www.qca.org.uk/qca_16908.aspx (last updated 21 April 2008).

QCA (2007c) *Learning that Lasts a Lifetime*. Available at http://www.qca.org.uk/ qca_16906.aspx (last updated April 2008).

Quicke, J. (1992) Pupil culture and the curriculum. *Westminster Studies in Education* 17, pp. 5–18.

Quicke, J. and Winter, C. (1993) Teaching the language of learning: towards a metacognitive approach to pupil empowerment. *Paper presented at BERA Liverpool*.

Qvortrup, J. (1990) A voice for children in statistical and social accounting: a plea for children's right to be heard. In James, A. and Prout, A. (eds) *Constructing and Reconstructing Childhood*. London: Falmer Press.

Roberts, P. (2006) *Nurturing Creativity in Young People*. A report to government to inform future policy. Nottingham: DfES and DCMS.

Rogers, C.R. (1970) Towards a theory of creativity. In Vernon, P.E. (ed.) *Creativity*. Harmondsworth: Penguin.

Rowland, S. (1987) Child in control: towards an interpretive model of teaching and learning. In Pollard, A. (ed.) *Children and Their Primary Schools*. Lewes: Falmer Press.

Rudduck, J. (2006) The past, the papers and the project. *Educational Review* 58(2), 131–143.

Rudduck, J. and Flutter, J. (2000) Pupil participation and pupil perspective: 'carving a new order of experience'. *Cambridge Journal of Education* 30(1), pp. 75–89.

Rudduck, J. and McIntyre, D. (2007) *Improving Learning through Consulting Pupils*. London: Routledge.

Rudduck, J., Chaplain, R. and Wallace, G. (1996) *School Improvement: What Can Pupils Tell Us?* London: David Fulton.

Rudduck, J., Demetriou, H., Myers, K., Fielding, M., Bragg, S., Arrot, M., McIntyre, D., Pedder, D., Reay, D. and MacBeath, J. (2004) *Consulting Pupils about Teaching and Learning*. London: Pearson Publishing.

Seltzer, K. and Bentley, T. (1999) *The Creative Age*. London: Demos.

Short, G. and Carrington, B. (1987) Towards an anti-racist initiative in the all-white primary school: a case study. In Pollard, A. (ed.) *Children and Their Primary Schools*. Lewes: Falmer Press.

Sugrue, C. (1997) *Complexities of Teaching: Child-Centred Perspectives*. London: Falmer Press.

Tom, A. (1984) *Teaching as a Moral Craft*. New York: Longman.

Towler, L. and Broadfoot, P. (1992) Self-assessment in the primary school. *Educational Review* 44(2), pp. 137–151.

Trafford, B. (1993) *Sharing Power in Schools: Raising Standards*. Ticknall: Education Now.

Triggs, P. and Pollard, A. (1998) Pupil experience and a curriculum for life-long learning. In Richards, C. and Taylor, P.H. (eds) *How Shall We School Our Children? Primary Education and its Future*. London: Falmer Press.

Troman, G. and Woods, P. (2001) *Primary Teachers' Stress*. London: Routledge-Falmer.

Troman, G., Jeffrey, B. and Raggl, A. (2007) Creativity and performativity policies in primary school cultures. *Journal of Education Policy* 22(5), 549–572.

Vygotsky, L. (1964) *Thought and Language*. Cambridge, Mass: MIT Press.

Vygotsky, L. (1978) The development of higher psychological processes. In Cole, M., Scribner, S., John-Steiner, V. and Souderman, E. (eds) *Mind in Society*. Cambridge, Mass: Harvard University Press.

Walker, R. (1989) The conduct of educational case studies: ethics, theory and procedures. In Hammersley, M. (ed.) *Controversies in Classroom Research (second edition)*. Buckingham: Open University Press.

Watts, M. and Bentley, D. (1991) Construction in the curriculum. Can we close the gap between the strong theoretical version and the weak version of theory in practice? *The Curriculum Journal* 2(2), pp. 171–182.

Webb, R. (1993) The National Curriculum and the changing nature of topic work. *The Curriculum Journal* 4(2), pp. 239–252.

Wegerif, R. (2002) *Thinking Skills, Technology and Learning*. London: The Open University.

Whistler, T. (1988) *Rushavenn Time*. Brixworth: Brixworth V.C. Primary School.

Winnicott, D.W. (1964) *The Child, the Family and the Outside World*. Harmondsworth: Penguin.

Woodhead, C. (1995) Annual Lecture of HM Chief Inspector of Schools, London.

Woods, P. (1990) *Teacher Skills and Strategies*. London: Falmer.

Woods, P. (1993) *Critical Events in Teaching and Learning*. London: Falmer Press.

Woods, P. (1994) Critical students: Breakthroughs in learning. *International Studies in the Sociology of Education* 4(2), pp. 123–146.

Woods, P. (1995) *Creative Teachers in Primary Schools*. Buckingham: Open University Press.

Woods, P. (2002) Teaching and learning in the new millennium. In Sugrue, C. and Day, C. (eds) *Developing Teaching and Teachers: International Research Perspectives*. London: Falmer, pp. 73–91.

Woods, P. and Jeffrey, B. (1996) *Teachable Moments: The Art of Creative Teaching in Primary Schools*. Buckingham: Open University Press.

Woods, P., Jeffrey, B., Troman, G. and Boyle, M. (1997) *Restructuring Schools, Reconstructing Teachers*. Buckingham: Open University Press.

Woods, P., Boyle, M. and Hubbard, N. (1999) *Multicultural Children in the Early Years: Creative Teaching, Meaningful Learning*. Clevedon: Multilingual Matters.

Wragg, E.C. (ed.) (2005) *Letters to the Prime Minister*. London: Central Books.

Wragg, T. (1995) First fruits of emancipation. *The Times Educational Supplement*, 10 February, p. 20.

Wragg, T. (2004) 'Introduction' to ESRC Creativity in Education Seminar. *Creative Teaching and Learning*. University of Exeter.

Young, M. (1999) Knowledge, learning and the curriculum of the future. *British Education Research Journal* 25(4), pp. 463–477.

Zimiles, H. (1987) Progressive education: on the limits of evaluation and the development of empowerment. *Teachers College Record* 89(2), pp. 201–217.

Index